The Maturing Church

Langham
GLOBAL LIBRARY

The Maturing Church

An Integrated Approach to Contextualization,
Discipleship and Mission

Ermias G. Mamo

Langham

GLOBAL LIBRARY

© 2017 by Ermias G. Mamo

Published 2017 by Langham Global Library
An imprint of Langham Creative Projects

Langham Partnership
PO Box 296, Carlisle, Cumbria CA3 9WZ, UK
www.langham.org

ISBNs:
978-1-78368-365-9 Print
978-1-78368-374-1 ePub
978-1-78368-375-8 Mobi
978-1-78368-376-5 PDF

British Library Cataloguing in Publication Data
A catalogue record for this book is available from the British Library

ISBN: 978-1-78368-365-9

Cover & Book Design: projectluz.com

Dedication

To Lalekeno Sula (my mother), and
Amarech Milkyas (my wife) –
two ladies who contributed a lot to my discipleship journey.

CONTENTS

Preface

In my twenty years of full-time ministry, I have observed changes in the ministry of the church as it is influenced by the change of the culture. To begin with my own context, it has been more than two decades now since the downfall of the Marxist regime in Ethiopia. It is a different season with different challenges. Though the church in Ethiopia has gone through a series of persecutions (Italian invasion, Marxist regime . . .) currently, it is experiencing relative freedom of worship and evangelization. The church that met under the Marxist regime in small groups in individuals' living rooms and bedrooms is now out in public using stadiums and holding open-air meetings; there is no intimidation and no imprisonment. Dark days are gone for evangelicals. Numerically, the insignificant evangelical minority are now claiming approximately twenty million believers; that is about 20 percent of the total population. Evangelicals who were treated as second-class citizens are now given key positions in the government as faithful civil servants. They are granted the right to build church facilities, and confiscated properties have been returned to churches. More than at any other time the churches are involved in community service and development projects. For those of us who lived through the dark days it is a miracle to see the church come to this stage. With the fast-growing churches and population explosion, Ethiopia is expected to be one of the new mission centers for the global church.

Unfortunately, not all the changes have brought positive results. With the freedom of religion and worship, all sorts of negative cultural influences have infiltrated the church. In its spiritual journey, the church has faced numerous obstacles. The church that stuck together in those dark days and united to the same cause began to disintegrate. Believers and church leaders took each other as far as the courts, to the extent that it brought public embarrassment to the church. Christian public officers have proved to be as corrupt as non-believers, which discredited the witness of Christianity. Believers divided and fought on ethic and language issues. Independent churches mushroomed and prosperity gospel preachers multiplied everywhere. False teachers and prophets ravaged the church. The evangelical church that strongly defended the brutal Marxist regime gave in to entertaining the devil and lost its testimony before the unbelieving world. Ministers who sacrificially served the church now opened their own churches where they could reign above all and take control of the leadership.

As I began to research and read extensively, I realized that the problem is not just Ethiopian, but it is African and it is global. For the global church leaders and ministers, the lingering questions are, what is going on? and what can be done to bring the church back on the right track? This book is not just an academic exercise; it is my passion and my heart outpoured. It is reflective, informative and directive. It is for leaders, for educators and for all people of God who desire to see the church restored to its God-given position.

The book is an attempt to map out the challenges of the global church in regard to discipleship. It proposes possible directions towards solving the problem with an integrative approach that brings contextualization, discipleship and mission together. It offers a theoretical foundation with practical strategies for effective discipleship that contributes to the mission of the global church. The key concept of the study is the integration of contextualization and discipleship in the maturing process of the global church, in order to do mission. The integrated approach focuses on the contextual presentation of the gospel, the transformation of lives, and the formation of kingdom community as key issues in the process. After presenting in the preface the need for an integrated approach to mature the church, I outline my own personal journey that includes how I got saved and discipled, to underline the need for discipleship and mentoring. The first chapter begins with identifying the internal and external challenges faced by the global church, followed by a chapter that establishes the biblical and theological foundations for contextualized discipleship for mission. In the third and fourth chapters I present the core message of the book, the integration of contextualization and discipleship towards maturing the body of Christ. Chapter 5 discusses the specific context of Ethiopian evangelical churches in relation to contextualized discipleship that can be mirrored for churches in other contexts. The sixth chapter gives strategic direction to practical steps in integrating discipleship into different ministries of the church. Chapter 7 concludes with recommendations for the future journey of the global church in disciple making.

The following figure helps to capture the concept of his integration more vividly. Contextualization is about effective communication of the gospel, which is what the church has been commissioned to do. The mission of the church is primarily to make disciples of all nations and so advance the kingdom of God. In other words, the church is called and commissioned to proclaim a contextualized gospel, to initiate believers by rituals, and to form a community that will continue to serve together in unity. In this integrated approach, the focus is to establish mission as an identity of the church not just as one of the activities. Furthermore, the testimony of the church is to become comprehensive and integrated in sharing life, not just words.

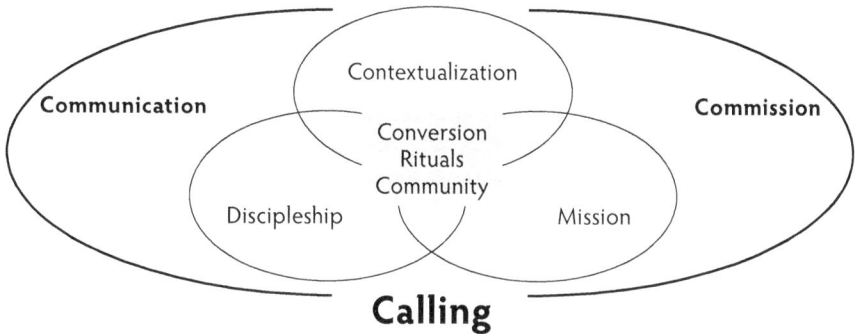

Figure 1. Integration of Contextualization and Discipleship

This is a critical juncture in the history of global Christianity. It is necessary to think about its future, for two reasons. First, it is a reality today that the center of Christianity is shifting from the northern hemisphere to the southern. Churches in the non-West are growing while their counterparts in the West are declining due to the influence of growing secularism and postmodern culture. However, before one comes to conclusions about the movement of the center of gravity to the non-Western churches it is important to check the foundation of the new centers. Without firm foundations in the Word of God, discussions about new centers are not realistic. For instance, churches in Africa are struggling because of lack of discipleship. With believers added daily but with no strong discipleship in place it is difficult to produce mature believers. Ethnic conflicts continue to claim lives, and poverty is deepening as the church boasts about the number of converts to Christianity. Preaching a gospel that does not transform lives and bring changes in the community fails to convince people. To be effective the gospel has to be both preached and lived. The church has to become a disciple-making church before it becomes a missionary-sending church. Otherwise, it will be multiplying syncretistic and nominal religion that does not serve the eternal purpose of God. E. Ashford is right when he writes, "Nominal Christianity is a bankrupt religion; it may have the Bible, cross on the top of meeting houses, and even the name Christian, but its adherents are not saved."[1] In fact, an unsaved person is not qualified to be a missionary. The non-Western churches have to deal with the discipleship issues in order to be ready for their role in global Christianity. Effective discipleship not only matures the members of the church but also equips them to present the gospel in words and deeds.

Second, this is an opportune time to discuss an integrated approach because currently many theologians and church leaders notice the issue of discipleship as a key missing link in the mission endeavor of the church. Edgemon writes, "For many years evangelism has received more attention than discipleship, but today there is a renewed concern for discipleship and equipping ministry . . . This emphasis has increased appreciably during the last fifteen years."[2] Moreover, currently there are significant practical moves towards discipling the nations. One of those movements is the "Disciple Africa" movement started by the Ethiopian Kale Heywet Church (EKHC) partnered by SIM. It is a young movement but it is growing and spreading throughout Africa with a vision of the global church. There are also other local, global, and parachurch organizations that are investing in discipleship and related ministries of the church.

Therefore, this study is part of what is already fermenting in the hearts and lives of many leaders. My intention is not only to collaborate with those who hold a similar vision but also to offer a reflective and integrative dimension to what is already underway. The issue of discipleship is the cry of genuine members, leaders and ministers of Christ globally. One of the ways to keep the global church of Christ alive and active in advancing the kingdom of God is through contextualized discipleship. Every discipleship journey begins with personal salvation and I would like to begin this book with my own story of salvation and discipleship. This is a small example of the journeys experienced by many disciples in the body of Christ. God's miraculous intervention in my life and his providence in difficult times proves the need for God's grace in our spiritual journey.

---

1. Ashford, *Theology*, 191.

2. Edgemon, "Evangelism," 539. Kenneth Chafin in 1966 observed the increased attention to discipleship and since then there has been a continued emphasis on discipleship until these days with many books and articles being published. Books on discipleship include *Relevant Indigenous Disciple-Making* (Motty), *Discipleship in the 21st Century Mission* (Park and Eom, eds.), and *Traditioning Disciples* (Mallon) just to mention a few of the current publications.

Acknowledgements

The book is not only a product of my research interest, but also it is my vision and burden that the Lord has placed on my heart. Therefore, first and foremost, I am grateful to my God and Savior for his grace in guiding and enabling me to share my passion with other servants of the kingdom of God.

I would also like to thank institutions for their various contributions in seeing this book come to publication. Langham Partnership, Asbury Seminary, Fuller Seminary, and Ethiopian Graduate School of Theology all played a crucial role in facilitating my sabbatical research.

I would like to appreciate individuals who stood beside me to encourage me and support me in whatever they could. Dr Stuart Rochester, who corrected and edited the manuscript, Drs Judy & Sherwood Lingenfelter, who hosted me during my stay at Fuller Seminary, and Dr Tesfaye Yacob, who always encouraged me in my studies – these all deserve my deepest gratitude.

Last, but not least, my appreciation goes to my family: to my wife Amarech for her prayers, to my son Ephrem and his wife Rose for their encouragement, to my daughters Metasebia and Amen for their laughter and sense of humour when I got bored with the writing, and of course, to my autistic son Nathan for his reminder of discipleship in the context of suffering which can never be appreciated enough.

List of Figures

List of Abbreviations

ECFE   Evangelical Churches Fellowship of Ethiopia

ECWA   Evangelical Church of West Africa

EOTC   Ethiopian Orthodox Tewahido Church

EECMY   Ethiopian Evangelical Church Mekane Yesus

EKHC   Ethiopian Kale Heywet Church

FDRE   Federal Democratic Republic of Ethiopia

KHC   Kale Heywet Church

SIM   Sudan Interior Mission, now Serving in Mission

My Personal Discipleship Journey: Saved and Discipled

Southern Ethiopia is the home of many tribes and ethnic groups. Being on the periphery for centuries, it has received little or no attention from the central government. Before Menelik II's incorporation of the southern region, traditional chiefs and kings administered it. The Aari, one of the southern people groups, are located in the Southern Omo region, where the main administrative town is called Jinka. The Aari, according to the recent census, number about 212,000 people.[1] They are mainly subsistence farmers. Before the arrival of the missionaries most Aari practiced traditional religion and a few were Orthodox believers. The first missionaries arrived in 1954 at Bako, then the administrative center of the region. They began their ministry with Ethiopian evangelists preaching the gospel in market places and public gatherings. Today most of the Aari people have heard the gospel and a little more than a quarter are professing evangelical believers.

Mamo Guisha, my father, was born in one of the Aari villages called Sheppe. As a son of a farmer he was expected to get married and settled at an early age. But he was a bit prodigal and became a village gang member. He robbed people and did other bad things. He also persecuted and threatened early converts to Christianity in the village. One day it dawned on him that he was getting old without having a child. The culturally accepted age for marriage in those days was fifteen for men and thirteen for girls. He was way beyond this age and it began to concern him. Finally, he decided to get married, but because of his age he thought it would be good to marry a divorcee or steal a wife from a polygamous husband. Because divorce is forbidden in the culture his only choice was a married woman. My mother, the third living wife of her polygamous husband, was already married with two children when my father began to show interest in her. One day she had a fight with her husband. She got mad and began walking to her parent's home. She suddenly met my father at a crossroad, where he took a knife out of his pocket and proposed, "Will you marry me?" It might seem like a nightmare, but that was their wedding day. So, scared for her life, she agreed to marry him and they ran away to a far village in fear of her previous husband. My

---

1. Federal Democratic Republic of Ethiopia Population Census Commission 2008, 78.

mother tried to run away a few times but when she realized she was pregnant she stopped her attempts.

They began a new life working for people for their daily bread. When my mom gave birth to my older brother, my father was so happy. However, that joy was short-lived. The baby got sick when he was only two months old. According to the traditional approach, my father went to the witch doctor to inquire the cause of the sickness. The reply from the witch doctor was that his ancestors were not happy with him and he had to offer sacrifices and gifts to appease them. He even went on to say he would never have children if he failed to bring the sacrifices. My father, puzzled by the request, and knowing that they could not afford the request, thought the ancestor would understand him. Soon my older brother died. They were heartbroken. My father's dream of having children was shattered. Life moved on and they had me a year later. However, while they were still rejoicing, I became sick at the same age as my older brother. My father visited the witch doctor for a second time and received the same response. Desperate and helpless, my father shared the situation with my mother. My mother cried the whole day as she held me in her arms. I was seriously sick. My parents were desperate. It was the lowest moment of their lives.

Right about nightfall, a lady from the neighborhood rushed in. She was a friend of my mother's. She apologized for not coming earlier as she had spent the whole day in the field planting crops. She asked my mother how I was doing. My mother replied, "I don't think he will make it tonight, he is dying." The woman felt so sad and cried with my mother for some time. Then she said to my mother, "You know three days ago there was this man who told us about a new religion which we are part of now. Would you try it? It is about Jesus Christ. You never know, you might get help." My mother, who was disappointed with all the requirements of the ancestors, replied, "How much do they charge? Can we afford it? Can it save my dying child?" The lady replied, "This religion is for free and I think it is worth trying; if you get help you keep on believing, if it doesn't you can quit." Without being sure about the outcome, my mother decided to try it. The woman went home promising to come in the morning and to lead them to Christ. When my father came home, she shared what the woman told her and they decided to become Christians. That very night about midnight, God miraculously healed me, her dying child. God sent his healing power even before they made an official commitment of their lives to Christ. In the morning, the woman came with her husband and my parents came to Christ. To this day, my mother's memories are fresh and she is thankful for God's grace that intervened in her life.

God saved me miraculously and I grew up in a Christian family. When Marxism came to power in Ethiopia, I was a young lad. The government closed the churches before I really captured the truth of the gospel. The elders and pastors of the churches joined the Communist party and the churches were left without leaders. Being one of the few literate young people in the whole village, I was often asked to read the Bible in church. No expositions, no comments. I read the Bible, a chapter at a time! But I was not free of the negative impact of the regime. My own father, who used to be a church leader, added two more wives. Our sweet home became chaotic. He started drinking, coming home late, and abusing my mother. He was a caring husband and a loving father to us before he became involved in the political leadership. Then everything changed: our evening devotions turned into evening fights, and lovely conversation turned into long arguments and bitter exchanges. Our loud laughter around the cooking fire disappeared and was replaced by tears of distress. My little brother and I were deeply affected by the painful situation especially after we learned that our parents were contemplating divorce. We resented the Marxist regime and doubted the authenticity of Christianity.

As we struggled through, I finished high school and joined a teacher's training school far away from where my parents lived. Though my father had backslidden, my mother always encouraged us to keep the faith in Christ and prayed for us continually. Despite the family crisis, there was always a morning prayer and an evening devotion. She at times forced us to read the Scriptures. As an illiterate mother, she told us stories of God's miraculous intervention in her life that remains within us until today. When I joined the training college, I thought that was a good opportunity for me to explore the world and see what I had missed so far. After a month or two at the training center, God connected me with a friend who changed my life for good. I met him through another friend. One afternoon, after a warm Ethiopian greeting and chat, he asked me, "Have you been baptized by the Holy Spirit?" Baffled, I thought of water baptism and answered, "Yes, I do take communion!" He knew that I did not understand him and since that day he became a mentor and friend to me. He prayed with me, discussed different issues, corrected me when I was wrong, and encouraged me. About seven months after we met, I found myself transformed from the inside out. My spiritual grounding was strong; it became a turning point in my life. The stories my mother shared with us, and the mentoring done by my friend, led me to a fresh experience of God. I resisted persecution from the Marxist cadres with great joy at the training center and thereafter.

In retrospect, I recall two key things that took place in my spiritual development. First, family-based discipleship served as a backbone for my spiritual journey. My mother was my primary mentor and model in my early days of physical and spiritual formation. Family as a discipleship center was a contextualized approach for a persecuted community. As churches were closed, the only place we had to get our spiritual tutoring was at home. Second, my friend, who was a fellow student, came close to disciple me and walked with me as I grew in Christ. He strengthened my fledgling faith in the face of persecution and adversity. He pointed me to Christ rather than demanding that I copy him. He patiently waited for the Spirit of the Lord to work in my life in his time. He created an environment for my spiritual growth. I was bold enough to witness about Christ and took abuse from the director of the institution for the sake of Christ. After my graduation, I was ready to disciple others and I finally ended up becoming a full-time minister. During the brutal Marxist persecution, I had an opportunity to grow in Christ because of discipleship that fit the context. Not just myself, but the entire believing community grew stronger in suffering.

Introduction

The philosophers have only interpreted the world, in various ways.
The point, however, is to change it. – Karl Marx

Marx dreamed of changing the world as he criticized the philosophers. His attempt to change the world failed because humanity does not have the power and the knowledge to change the world. There have been many philosophers and politicians who have promised to change the world, but they have failed to live up to their words. The problem of the world is not just a system – it is sin. The systems are twisted because human beings are sinful. The social classes are created as a result of the sinful and selfish nature of humanity. Unlike the philosophers' theories, Christianity is not about interpreting the world, it is about transforming the world. That is what Christ has done and what he has commanded the church to do. Christianity is more than individual salvation and success; it is working towards bringing the kingdom of God on earth as it is in heaven. Believers are saved by God's grace to become salt and light in their world, to bring an eternal hope to those who are dying without hope. Christians are the change agents whom God has placed here on earth.

Unfortunately, the reality we experience in our world today is different from the expectation set by God for believing communities. The world is challenging and scolding the church in its failure to model the kingdom life. The church that is expected to demonstrate the love of Christ to the world struggles to have unity among its members. Ethnocentrism and denominationalism are destroying the kingdom of God. In the words of the Hirschs, religion can either make us good or very, very bad,[1] because if there is no internal transformation, becoming a religious zealot creates more dissension than unity. The Hirschs, quoting C. S. Lewis, continued, "If the divine does not make us better, it will make us very much worse. Of all the bad men, religious bad men are the worst."[2] When we try to witness about our life in Christ, the world rebukes us for our hypocrisy. They question our authenticity and point to the logs in our eyes (Matt 7:3).

In my judgment the global church is currently facing its worst enemy. It is subtle and encroaching step by step from the least expected angle to destroy the

---

1. Hirsch and Hirsch, *Untamed*, 59.
2. Ibid., 60.

church. It was a challenge for believers in the early days of Christianity, it is a challenge today, and it will be in the future. This enemy is lack of discipleship – a lack of an organized effort to turn mere members into disciples of Christ. It is killing the church in the West and the church in the non-West is seriously sick of it. Many leaders and theologians have pointed to the problem in recent times. In the article "Deepening the Bonds of Christian Community," Jim Courson writes these opening words about the church in Asia:

> From a discipling standpoint, the church in Taiwan is in crisis. Two problems plague protestant churches of all denominations. One is the low rate at which new believers are incorporated into the church. A study conducted by Lutheran missionary Allen J. Swanson during the decade of the 1970s showed the net gain of one for every 25 "decisions" . . . A second equally disturbing problem is the high loss rate among new Christians. For every three new converts brought into church membership by baptism, two will be lost within a short period of time.[3]

If the conversion rate is dropping and of the few converts the majority are retreating back to their old lifestyle, there is a serious problem. As missiologists have concluded, the church in Asia is one of the new centers of global Christianity. If the reality on the ground is otherwise, the church needs to seriously examine the issue and deal with it before it is too late.

An African church leader's reflection on the issue of discipleship reports a similar situation: "I can go out in any day and make as many converts as time permits. It is easy to organize congregations. My problem is not evangelism; it is discipling. While lots of new believers enter in the front door of the church, too many leave by the back."[4] All the exciting numerical growth of the church in Africa can truly be celebrated if members become disciples. However, the reality in Africa is that thousands decide to follow Christ, but on account of the lack of discipleship many backslide, and others live a double life that dishonors God. When there is a lack of discipleship Christianity withers before it takes root. Joseph Galgalo's observation about the church in Africa indicates this reality. He writes,

---

3. Courson, "Deepening the Bonds," 301. Courson's study is based on Swanson's ("Decision or Disciples?," 54) research in Taiwanese churches on the problem of "lasting converts." He points out that one of the major barriers is the inability of the churches to keep their converts, which clearly indicates a serious problem of discipleship in the churches. For more information, see Allen Swanson's *Mending the Nets*.

4. Zahniser, *Symbol*, 6.

African Christianity definitely carries the 'Christian' labels but has a lot of the African traditional religious beliefs and practices in its content. The Bible, catechesis, paraphernalia, liturgies, rites, and Christian terminology such as incarnation, redemption, new birth, resurrection, heaven and hell are used. Despite the domestication and usage of these concepts, conceptual differences between Christian doctrines and traditional understanding abound. The differences often reveal a clear dichotomy and sometimes even contradiction between faith claims and ethical or moral applications. Also, faith or theological imperative often is secondary to any social demand.[5]

Galgalo points out two crucial defects in African Christianity. First, little or no transformation of minds or values is taking place. Christianity has not changed the worldview of the believers but it has taught a new language without transforming lives. Second, Christianity has failed to bring behavioral change in the believers. The cultural thoughts and practices go on underneath as members claim to be Christians. When there is lack of discipleship, churches cannot keep their converts – which clearly indicates a serious problem of discipleship in the churches. There is always a discrepancy between the doctrine and the practice, the beliefs and the behaviors, the claims and the reality. It is easy to learn Christian expressions and apply Christian labels, but true Christianity requires more than the external cover-ups. It demands a decision to follow Christ daily, carrying the cross.

Two of the largest and fastest growing churches in Africa are located in Nigeria and Ethiopia. The leaders of those churches are not happy with the current reality of the churches. The leader of ECWA, one of the largest denominations in Nigeria, writes, "ECWA is not a disciple-making, but a convert-making church."[6] In other words, people are invited to join the church membership but not to be citizens in the kingdom of God. The result is always devastating for the witness of the church. Along the same lines, one of the prominent leaders of the church in Ethiopia, Ato Shiferaw W. Michael, describes the status of the church as follows:

> . . . seemingly there is an explosive growth, but it is obesity; there is colorfulness but in many senses it is external; there is visible affection, but it is superficial, not from the heart; supposedly there

---

5. Galgalo, *African Christianity*, 2.

6. Motty, *Indigenous Christian*, 29.

is submissiveness but as long as one's view is accepted; there is a tolerance, but only temporary; there is worship, but with no sign of the fear of God; there is religiosity but it is not substantiated with testimony.[7]

The leaders' critical comments point out that the numerical growth of the church is on shaky ground and the spirituality is external and superficial. It might seem harsh criticism but it points to the serious outcomes of lack of biblical discipleship. Believers fail not only to display a genuine Christian life but also destroy the witness of the church before the watching world. What else can be more disconcerting than this problem? If the church fails to make disciples it means it will also fail to effectively accomplish its mission. Lack of disciples in the church will hurt the mission of the church altogether.

Non-Western churches are not suffering alone, for the churches in the West are sharing the same challenges. Writing about the church membership situation in America, a theology student puts it vividly: it is "the revolving door problem': as fast as new believers enter the front door, others leave out the back."[8] It is a big loss when converts come to the church and then leave. Worse, though, is that people who claim to be Christians fail to bear spiritual fruit and become obstacles to non-believers coming to Christ. In other words, converts become nominal Christians with a secular mindset. Henry Schmidt reports,

> In 1977 a Dutch telecaster asked Dr Billy Graham, "We read about all the people in America being born again, that this was the year of the evangelicals, that thousands – perhaps millions – are coming to Christ, yet we also see in America abortion on the increase, deterioration of the family structure, the crime rate increasing. How is it that so many can be born again and your society be so sick?"[9]

It is a challenging question not just for leaders like Billy Graham, but for all believers in all generations. Such critical questions from the world around should lead the church to a soul-searching inquiry to locate the missing aspect of Christianity. Schmidt adds, "Religion is increasing its influence in society but morality is losing its influence. The secular world would seem to offer abundant evidence that religion is not greatly affecting our lives."[10]

---

7. Bekele, *In-Between People*, 185.

8. Zahniser, *Symbol*, 15.

9. Schmidt, *Conversion*, 107.

10. Ibid.

The church is losing its people and its influence in the world. If the back doors of the church continue to be open, the loss will continue. The global church has to step up not only to keep the believers in, but also to mature them in Christ to affect their world. The mortality rate for new converts is high. If half of the people who join a church each year fail to follow through and develop as disciples, the church must accept responsibility for this failure. "If we treated newborn babies as carelessly as we treat newborn Christians, the mortality rates would equal the appalling mortality of church members."[11] The members of the church are responsible to welcome, train and incorporate the new believers, otherwise our evangelism is in vain. Through discipleship, attitudes are corrected and behaviors are shaped. Discipleship on the one hand deals with immaturity of believers and on the other hand equips them to be witnesses to the world. Immature churches waste and abuse the gift of God, as was the case in the church at Corinth.

There are too many immature Christians. Churches are filled with spiritual infants. The Barna Research Group reveals that 50 percent of "born again" Christians have no idea what John 3:16 refers to. Many do not know the concept of the Great Commission or the gospel. You see, spiritual ignorance and biblical illiteracy are commonplace. People follow more popular views, seeking feeling and more experiences. Many are hungry for miracles, healings and spectacular wonders.[12]

The immaturity of the believers is exposed in their Scripture knowledge and in their relationship with the world and fellow believers. Immature believers tend to follow popular views and individuals rather than the guidance of the Scripture. Due to the immaturity of the church internal conflicts and false teachings torment the church from continent to continent. The prosperity gospel in Africa, secularism and nominalism in the West and other challenges in all other contexts test the strength of the church. Spiritual immaturity leads many people to seek entertainment rather than a deep teaching in Christ that promotes spiritual growth.

I could go on and on and mention issue after issue. The bottom line is that the global church is in a discipleship crisis. The problem may be manifesting itself differently in different contexts but the root cause is the same. Whether it is a leadership crisis, ethnocentrism, or nominalism, all have their roots in lack of authentic discipleship. The problem is fatal, the issue is serious and the

---

11. Edgemon, "Evangelism," 542.
12. Park and Eom, *Discipleship*, 78.

need is urgent. These challenges are not new for the global church. Since the beginning of the church in the apostolic period, the church has gone through internal and external challenges but it has come thus far by the grace of God. The challenges should not lead us to hopelessness but rather should awaken us to become actively engaged and to work towards empowering the church. The intention of this book is not to leave us wondering but to be informed and to be strategic and biblical in our witness and presence in the world as a body of Christ. As the challenges are multifaceted, our approach should be integrated and holistic.

1

The Need for an Integrated Approach

Christianity without the living Christ is inevitably Christianity without discipleship, and Christianity without discipleship is always Christianity without Christ. – Dietrich Bonhoeffer

Christianity is not a man-made religion. It is not an attempt by humanity to reach God, as is the case in all other religions. It is rather God's gracious move towards humanity even when humankind is running away from God. Christianity is Christ-centered rather than human-centered. We are saved by Christ through faith. But in the absence of discipleship it is easy to replace Christ by other material and liturgical traditions, forms and structures without the presence of Christ. Throughout the centuries the greatest challenge of the church has not been external persecutions but internal struggles which try to disconnect Christ, the head of the church, from the church, the body of Christ. The contemporary church of Christ is not different.

The fallen nature of humanity always fails to put God at the center. Sin has corrupted all aspects of humanity. The physical, intellectual and emotional desire of the natural man or woman is not to please God but rather to please self. Therefore, it takes continual training and discipline of minds, souls and bodies to bring humanity under the lordship of Christ. Spiritual growth requires continuous battle with our flesh and strong commitment to train ourselves in the things of God. As newborn babies grow in parental care and instruction, newborn believers need spiritual care from the community. The challenge facing the global church today with regard to discipleship is how to deal with three problems: the current membership-based approach of the church (making converts not disciples), overcoming cultural hostility towards discipleship, and the overwhelming presence of the world in the church, leading to incomplete mission.

Members not Disciples

Churches brag about their growth, which is based on the numerical increase of members. We are in an era where bigger is seen as better. Missionary reports generate funds if there is an increase in the number of converts. Pastors of megachurches are seen as successful because of the size of the congregation. Christianity is adopting the business model of the world and missing the basic teaching of Christ. However, the mission of the church is not to gather converts in a building – it is making disciples and building the kingdom of God. The attitude of the leaders and ministers has to change from boasting about members to making disciples.

When a person takes an initial step to follow Christ, it is in response to the work of the Spirit of God. It is the beginning of a new chapter that has to be engraved in everyday life. The spiritual journey continues, strengthened by the Holy Spirit, as the Word of God shapes the convert. Though conversion may be a one-time dramatic incident or a slow development, spiritual growth is a process. "Salvation costs you nothing, but discipleship costs you everything. Salvation occurs in a moment but discipleship takes a lifetime. Jesus asks whether or not you truly want to live a life of discipleship."[1] Mark Driscoll points out two things involved in discipleship: first, discipleship involves cost. It costs everything. It requires people to offer their lives to Christ and make him the Lord of their lives. Christ gave his life for us and we are expected to offer nothing less than our entire self. Second, it is a lifetime process. Discipleship is not a course that is offered for a semester or two. It is a lifetime learning and growing project. Christian living is a lifestyle where we are trained to think and act according to God's will.

During our time in Los Angeles, California, we had American friends who visited and had a meal with us. After having the spicy Ethiopian dish, our friends often asked for the recipe. My wife would answer, "I don't have a recipe," then they would ask, "How do you know how to make it?" Her response, "I just know it!" The recipe is not written on paper but written on her memory. Having the right information is one thing but training ourselves to practice it and live by it takes intentional discipline. The Christian life is beyond

---

1. Driscoll, *Who Do You Think*, 212.

memorizing verses; it is following Christ in our whole lives. As technology advances, many Christians have the Bible installed on their computers and mobile phones in multiple versions, but not in their lives. Believers watch preaching series on TV, read big volumes of commentaries on Scripture, and attend many revival meetings, without their personal lives being impacted. We live in an information age, but there is a big gap between what people know and how people live. As a result, people have become the center of their own lives rather than allowing Christ to be there. They obey and practice not what the Scripture is saying but what their flesh desires.

One of the factors contributing to the gap between knowledge and practice is the lack of emphasis on discipleship as a main goal in the lives of believers. Discipleship is a compulsory course for every Christian. It was requisite in the practice of the early church and it should be the same for the contemporary church. Yet the contemporary church has replaced discipleship with various activities in the church. For instance, in Africa, where churches are growing exponentially, discipleship is forgotten and replaced by religious experiences and charismatic practices. Believers are more interested in prophetic messages and healing services than strong discipleship-oriented teaching. Emotional experiences and exuberance in worship is the ultimate target of many church goers. The search for experiences is pushing Scripture from the center of Christianity and charismatic preachers are overshadowing Christ. The emotional experiences people seek fail to address deeper issues of community transformation. Galgalo rightly observes:

> At a deeper level Christianity has failed to inspire, reshape and transform African social history and basic identity. A glance through history may unravel why Christianity even though widely accepted and followed in Africa yet has remained a stranger within the phenomenal world of African religiosity.[2]

According to Galgalo, Christianity in Africa has failed to challenge, critique and transform the cultural status quo. Though they claim to be Christians the worldview of many believers is not shaped by the Scriptures. For some, Christianity provides a social affiliation rather than a transformation of life. Many pastors focus on material blessings and "success" as a sign of spiritual progress that takes the attention away from Christ. Churches are losing their uniqueness and becoming just human organizations with a human-centered approach. Small group meetings, Bible studies, and mentoring structures have

---

2. Galgalo, *African Christianity*, 7.

given way to church shopping and entertaining services. The current concern of churches seems mainly about membership and popularity. Believers travel miles to see charismatic preachers healing in open-air meetings but refuse to meet in small care groups. The focus is on being blessed, not on spiritual growth or maturity.

The dropping of discipleship from ministries of the church or giving it just a lip service has left Christianity in crisis. The uniqueness of Christianity depends not on the civilization of its culture or the size of its adherents but on its strong attachment to Christ and his presence among his people. The quality of the church should not be assessed by its fancy buildings and fantastic worship services but by how the community of believers acknowledges the lordship of Christ and witnesses his saving gospel in words and deeds. Christianity is about Christ and following him with commitment. It is about discipleship. As Bonhoeffer reminded us, "Christianity without discipleship is Christianity without Christ, and Christless Christianity is not Christianity at all."[3] The Scripture indicates that believers are attached to Christ as branches are attached to a vine. As the branches produce fruit as long as they stay on the vine, believers can only accomplish their mission by making Christ the center of their lives (John 15:1). To remain attached to the vine as a branch is the responsibility of disciples, so that they can be effective in their mission. The Gospel of John highlights the relationship between God and Jesus and Jesus and the followers of Jesus. Mission is a fruit of our relationship with God through Christ. At the closing of John's Gospel we read how Jesus asked Peter about his love for him and gave him the responsibility of keeping the sheep (John 21:15). Our mission has to be motivated and inspired by our love for our savior and redeemer. Not only has the focus of the churches moved away from discipleship but also the postmodern individualistic culture militates against discipleship.

Culture Hostile to Discipleship

The world we live in is changing. It is a globalized fast-paced world – a no delay, no waiting, quick fix and move on world. Take it easy! Enjoy yourself! No worries! These are the mottos of the day. It is an individualistic, egoistic and materialistic world. On one hand believers demand their rights from God when they face challenges; on the other hand, they don't like to be accountable

---

3. Bonhoeffer, *Cost.*

for a holy way of living. Rights are claimed but responsibilities are ignored. Our victory in Christ is overemphasized and the cross of Christ neglected as an old-fashioned thought. Unlike the early church, the culture shuns suffering and sacrificial living. The postmodern culture has disrupted discipleship in many ways. For instance, the "drive thru" and "MacDonaldized" culture is reflected in the believer's desire for instant transformation through magic prayer and anointed touch. It is about special anointing and experience rather than continuous and intentional building of spiritual lives. Discipleship is not an in-and-out process as the culture assumes. It takes time and commitment. The focus on entertainment and an easy life is also part of the cultural influence. The search for shortcuts and a suffering-free life prioritizes self at any cost.

One of the ways to encounter the challenge of the secularized culture is to obey Christ in discipling the nations. Unless we equip our members to follow Christ daily in their lives "weekend Christianity" cannot win the battle against anti-Christian cultural forces. Every context and every culture poses different challenges to believers, and so discipleship should be contextualized in response to the culture-specific threats. Christ proposed making disciples of every nation to resist the ever-increasing hostility to the people of God. Discipleship empowers a believer to properly handle the daily challenges of life. Discipleship is not an alternative given to the church to use if other things fail to work. It is a command given by the founder of the church, Jesus Christ. Joe Kapolyo is right when he writes, "The Great Commission is given by the highest authority in the universe, and it is binding on all disciples for all times. No other task comes with the same authority, the same universal scope or the same eternal consequence."[4] The contemporary church has its priorities mixed up. Issues that have to be tabled in every discussion of church leadership meetings are not getting the attention they deserve. Influenced by the cultural mindset, material things with no eternal values are prioritized at the expense of the main calling of the church. Making disciples of all nations is given to the church by the highest authority, Christ the head of the church. Our responsibility to share the gospel is not over when we bring people to Christ. We are called to make disciples. "Believers in Jesus are to train those with whom they have shared the gospel and led to the Lord. They are to do 'follow-up.' They are not to leave converts to Christ unchurched, untrained, and undiscipled."[5] The abandoned

---

4. Kapolyo, "Matthew," 5.
5. Wilder, "Biblical Theology," 5.

converts whom the church has failed to train properly will damage the witness and the health of the church.

Diminishing Community Influence

The church is called to influence the world as light and salt as it works towards the coming of the kingdom of God. The church serves as a transformation agent and models genuine community to the society. In the world where we witness crisis after crisis every day, whether it is natural or man-made, terrorism or ethnic conflicts claiming thousands of lives, what is the role of global Christians? The questions many people wonder about include these: How much is expected of Christianity in a society? Is the world irreparably damaged? Haven't things gotten out of control? If we dare to make a difference in our world where do you start – with individuals, structures, systems or cultures? Is a disciple of Christ responsible to tackle social evils beyond just offering prayers? The question of our involvement in our existing socio-political context has been a challenging question throughout the centuries. Sometimes the church has become too involved in the world and lost its prophetic voice. At the other extreme some believers isolate themselves in a ghetto, where they enjoy each other's company but lose their passion for the dying world.

Christianity is not a faith that keeps people in their caves just to meditate. It demands more than reflection – it demands action. It is a dynamic, transforming and public faith. Our involvement in a society matters for the ministry of the gospel. For instance, southern Ethiopia is probably the most evangelized part of Ethiopia, with the majority of its residents being evangelical Christians. Hawassa, the capital city, is arguably one of the most Christianized cities in Ethiopia. The zonal government administrative positions are mainly occupied by evangelical Christians. By some estimates, about 75 percent of people in government leadership are evangelical Christians. But in regard to corruption and embezzlement it is not different from other zones in Ethiopia, perhaps even worse. When challenged, many Christian government officials reply, "It is the system; you can't bring change unless you change the whole system, which is impossible."[6] But behind all the excuses lies the fear of facing the corrupted system. Thousands of believers lose their faith in the political process as they get overwhelmed by the corrupt structure. As the Ethiopian proverb goes,

---

6. Because of their experience in the past, and with the current situation of Christians in politics, many evangelicals are not interested in politics.

"Salt went to fetch water and ended up losing itself." Many believers are not sufficiently equipped to deal with such challenges let alone to influence others. When the church loses its public witness and credibility, its very existence comes into question. If the church loses its relevance and leadership in the community, then it loses its purpose for existence as a church.

If the church is not the salt and light of the world, then what is the church for? If believers withdraw from the political arena of this world, how do they demonstrate the justice and peace of God? We are called to advance the kingdom of God not just in its spiritual sense but in its entirety. If our message is not lived out, how can the world hear the message and follow Christ? These are questions that believers in every context have to think about critically, otherwise the world will continue to influence the church. Actually, the culture and the secular ideas have already been imbedded in our relationships and organizational structures. If we stay defensive, the world will infiltrate our churches before we know it. The church needs an offensive strategy built on strong discipleship. Influence requires more than verbal proclamation. It requires missional presence in the dying world.

Landa Cope argues that the reason behind all the Mosaic laws and instructions for the Israelites in the wilderness was to show that God is concerned with the transformation of the whole community rather than just the salvation of individuals.[7] According to Cope, Moses was a disciple maker. His calling was to make disciples out of Israelites so they could in turn model the life of God's people in discipling the nations as they observed and experienced the lives of God's people. He was assigned not only to facilitate the presence of God among the Israelites but also to bring peace and justice among the Israelites as they continued their journey to the Holy Land. It was a holistic discipleship. Beyond the spiritual presence among the nations they were called to reflect God's character in every dimension of life. However far the world is corrupted in its cultures and structures, it should not thwart our calling as believers to engage with it, challenge it and bring the light of the gospel. Jesus promised to be with us until the end of the age. Cope in her article published under the title "His Kingdom Come" contends that though Africa south of Sahara is mostly evangelized, the gospel has failed to transform traditional and cultural worldviews because of lack of discipleship. She writes:

> [In Africa] there are hundreds of thousands of churches and evangelists. It is the most Christianized continent in the world, if

---

7. Cope, *Introduction.*

you are looking at saved people. But does it fit any of the criteria for a blessed nation, as defined by God? The answer is no. In fact, thirty of the forty poorest countries of the world are in this region. God is wanting to teach us how to disciple nations.[8]

Of course, material wealth should not be taken as the only sign of being a Christian nation, but justice, peace and good governance are the fruits of Christian community. Christianity cannot achieve the desired transformation in the society without discipleship. Contextual discipleship equips believers to respond to the ailing world with compassion and action. In the discipleship process believers intentionally become involved and influence their world for Christ.

In the New Testament Jesus expected the fruits of transformed lives. He said, "Bear fruit in keeping with repentance" (Luke 3:8). The preaching of the gospel goes hand in hand with the transformation of communities. The life touched by the love of Christ spills its joy to others. The internal transformation of an individual manifests itself externally in serving the community. David Joel Hamilton summarizes as follows:

> Jesus' final words show us that he desires that every individual be redeemed and every society be transformed by the message of the gospel and the power of the Spirit. While the former requires urgent action to make sure the gospel is preached to all during our lifetime, the latter gives us the reason to plan multigenerational strategies which will transform communities and peoples.[9]

The way we disciple the nations should include both the preaching of the word and the modeling of Christian living. The world needs us. We are responsible to work towards the coming of God's kingdom with its justice and peace. Our failure to impact our world for Christ is inexcusable because we have been given the resources to influence our world. These spiritual resources if used properly foster maturity and mission. Discipleship begins with understanding the gospel and then living a Christ-like life in our context: that is contextualized discipleship. Scott Moreau argues that contextualization has to move beyond the foundational level towards the transformation of a society. He writes,

---

8. Cope, "His Kingdom Come" in Stier and Poor, *His Kingdom Come*, 43.
9. Stier and Poor, *His Kingdom Come*, 52.

. . . the biblical message is clear that God is deeply concerned for justice in every human society, we must also pay attention to areas within cultures that are in need of Kingdom-based social change or transformation, and consider what role local believers might have in facilitating that change as a sign to the rest of the society that the kingdom of God is in their midst.[10]

According to Moreau, contextualization should not limit itself to dealing with concepts and ideas but it should work on social change that affects the wider community. This is not an easy task. It takes an intentional and integrated approach to equip the church to live beyond and above the challenges. It is obvious that there is a great need for an integrated approach to contextualized discipleship to transform individual lives and the entire community. Our mission is incomplete if it fails to make disciples who can transform their communities.

Incomplete Mission

In the book of Acts, Jesus said to his disciples, "But you will receive power when the Holy Spirit has come upon you, and you will be my witnesses in Jerusalem and in all Judea and Samaria, and to the ends of the earth" (1:8). Christ promised the Holy Spirit to empower the disciples to be witnesses because a witness needs to be authentic and trustworthy. The question then is, can an immature church become an effective witness? Without the infilling of the Holy Spirit can human beings effectively accomplish God's mission? J. Ingleby in his challenging book *Beyond Empire* raises similar questions about the churches in the southern hemisphere: "Have the churches in the South been fully redeemed from their colonial origins?"[11] His conclusion is no! One of the reasons for his doubt is the issue of discipleship. He writes about some of the motives of conversion in southern churches:

It is an additional twist that the visible side of my Christian life may have real benefits – it may win me esteem, may get me a job, and may promote me to leadership. So a gap can open up between what I call "membership" – an open belonging to the cause – and

10. Moreau, *Contextualization in World Missions*, 5.

11. Ingleby, *Beyond Empire*, 173.

"discipleship," by which I mean allowing God into my inner life so that he can control it, and then living with the consequences.[12]

If Christianity is about membership, affiliation and social mobility, it is not a biblical Christianity; it is rather a Christendom Christianity, or in Ingleby's words a "colonial Christianity." Ingleby questions the preaching of the gospel by Western missionaries as well as the response of the indigenous believers. He points to the non-contextualized gospel preached to Africans and the wrong motives for which Africans embraced the gospel as basic hindrances. However, both areas can be addressed through contextualized discipleship. It is not too late to work on equipping the church in the south for effective mission. The question will continue to be a question if the church in the south fails to address the issue of discipleship. For mission to be complete the converts have to become disciples. But this soul-searching question presented by Ingleby has to be taken seriously.

As history reminds us, the 1910 Edinburgh Missionary Conference was more concerned about the unreached world and sending missionaries while the foundation of Christianity in Europe was soon to be challenged by the bloody consecutive wars. The intention was to reach the unreached in the distant lands of Africa and Latin America as soon as possible, but no one had expected that European Christianity would go through such a hard time of conflicts and wars. The war distracted the church from its mission and confused believers about the future of Christianity. There is a lesson here for the contemporary church: that the geographical expansion of the churches has to be supported with theological depth to ensure the transformation of believers and their wider community. Without the strong foundation of discipleship it is difficult to achieve our plans for mission and evangelism. In addition, sending missionaries who are not disciples can bring more damage to the message than impacting lives.

By the same token, the church in Africa may boast about the numerical growth, but actually, without proper discipleship, let alone reaching others, the church should be concerned for its own spiritual decay and uncertain future. In our mission endeavor, both the lives and the words of believers should speak the message, otherwise one can destroy the other. The world witnessed so-called Christian communities explode into inhumane and horrible atrocities when Rwanda, the east African center of revival, turned to bloody genocide. The Lord's Resistance Army in Uganda, the Kenyan election crisis, and the

---

12. Ibid., 204.

ethnic conflicts in Sudan and Ethiopia, are all happening among people who claim that they are the Christian majority.

The quick growth of churches in Africa is both a blessing and a challenge. It is amazing how quickly the gospel spreads in sub-Saharan Africa. Kwiyani writes,

> The growth of Christianity in Africa in the twentieth century is nothing short of a miracle. Over five hundred million people have converted to Christianity in the space of one hundred years, with 80 percent of them converting after 1970. Never in the history of Christianity have so many people been converted in so short a time.[13]

Of course, it is a miracle to have so many people responding to the message of the gospel in such a short time period. The miracle will continue to be a miracle only if the church disciples the converts to make a difference in their communities. The exponential growth of churches with no discipleship system to accommodate it is one of the greatest weaknesses of African Christianity. A church that sees sixteen thousand conversions[14] a day can only be overwhelmed by these numbers and be forced to let many go by the backdoor or give shallow discipleship teaching that fails to transform. Our work is not over when we bring people to the fellowship of believers – it has just started.

What happened in many corners of Africa can be called mass conversion. But mass conversion is always a mixed blessing. First, it is challenging for discipleship. Ministers are forced to give mass instruction and mass baptism. Individual mentoring is impossible. That leads to believers hiding in the system or fellowship without being exposed to the truth of the gospel. Sometimes believers overemphasize their denominational affiliation more than their identity in Christ, and that creates conflicts among believers. Park and Eom highlight this problem:

> [Many Africans] who had embraced the "brand of Christianity" espoused by the missionary group that brought the gospel to them became "proud" members of such denominations and not necessarily committed disciples of Jesus Christ because of the emphasis on the denominational particularities which

---

13. Kwiyani, *Sent Forth*, 16.

14. Sunquist's estimate regarding the growth of the church in Africa (in *Unexpected*).

often segregated against fellow African believers of different denomination.[15]

The believers claimed their identity from their denominational affiliation rather than Christ who called them to eternal fellowship. The key identity of Christians and their purpose in life should be drawn from Christ. Denominational, ethnic and geographical identities should be secondary to our identity as disciples of Christ. But in mass conversion the ethnic or other identities take precedence. There is also a good chance that mass conversion spreads nominalism. Nominalism is an obstacle to the witness of the church because the church appears to be hypocritical and loses its integrity before the world. The seed of the gospel sown among the nations will fail to bear fruit if it lacks the care and watering it needs. Whether it is in Africa or in the rest of the world, nominalism is a challenge for the mission of the church. It is critical to equip the church to become mature so that it can be stable and consistent in its involvement in mission.

Second, mass conversion with lack of discipleship can lead to a double life: the public life is separated from the private. Galgalo's critique of the church in Africa is worth quoting here:

> Most African Christians are deeply connected with Christ and at the same time are at a distance from him. They belong to the church and yet at the same time are marginal and occasionally act and live as complete outsiders, with very little or no concern at all for church matters or teachings.[16]

The double life is a manifestation of immature faith. Believers often appear to be pious, demonstrating spiritual gifts and talents in the church, but their failure to be consistent outside makes people question their genuineness. The insider-outside identity of immature believers confuses not only the believing community but also the unbelievers who search for truth. The bottom line is that the global church desperately needs an integrated contextualized approach to discipleship, in order to make disciples of all nations and to influence the world around for Christ.

---

15. Park and Eom, *Discipleship*, 205.
16. Galgalo, *African Christianity*, 2.

The Need for an Integrative Approach

Though I mentioned several challenges facing the global church today, there are also tremendous opportunities that the church can take advantage of. In fact, the growth of the church in the non-Western world, the involvement of new churches in global mission and the impact of the non-Western believers in reviving the Western churches is monumental. The church is growing even in the resistant areas of the globe. It is encouraging to see Muslims convert to Christianity through vision and dreams. Furthermore, non-Western churches are passionately involved in mission. From the poverty-stricken areas of southern Ethiopia, missionaries are sent to Pakistan and India. Nigerian missionaries are effectively serving in Western countries including Ukraine, a former communist country. The world has felt the impact of non-Western believers through formal missionary work as well as through non-formal approaches such as immigration. This time begs for the integrative approach where the church can maximize its opportunities and minimize its challenges. The integration between contextualization and discipleship helps the church to communicate effectively and creates an environment for growth and transformation.

If non-Western churches are to become mature and to equip believers for global mission, they certainly need contextualized discipleship. Matthew Michael, in his article "African Theology and the Paradox of Missions," criticizes African theologians for not being practical and relevant. He writes, "Remarkably, it appears that the African theological discourse has endlessly preoccupied itself with discourses that have no direct relevance or significance to the actual contexts of missions despite its seemingly superficial or outward connection."[17] Michael's criticism has a point, though he might be a little harsh on theologians and missiologists without giving any credit for their effort to understand their contexts. His point is that the theological issues that come to the table for contextualization have to be relevant to the current contexts of the people. For example, with postmodernism and the influence of Western culture now shaping African societies, issues concerning ancestors may not resonate with the younger generation.

True contextualization must handle the contemporary issues that the current generation deals with. Michael is right when he comments on the contribution of theology to the immediate context of the people because discipleship is about living our daily lives in following Christ. His fear is,

---

17. Michael, "African Theology," 79.

though, that contextualization might misread the signs of the times and run behind actual reality by focusing on older issues. The theologian should have the capacity to discern both the social and spiritual context of the believer and of the wider community. This requires an integrated approach where contextualization and discipleship work hand in hand. The need for discipleship in the global church is obvious, but what do we mean by discipleship, and what theological foundations do we have to recommend to believers around the globe? These questions will be discussed next.

2

Biblical and Theological Foundations for Discipleship

Since the fall of humanity, the relationship between God and the universe, including humanity, has been strained. Humanity tried through religions and rituals to mend the relationship, but it was in vain. Genesis 12 begins with God's initiative in recreating the people of God for his purpose of restoring humanity to its original position at creation. God chose to recruit his followers not through rules and regulations but by befriending them and communicating his message. Abraham, the father of the people of God, was called from where he was worshipping other gods of the day. The gentle voice of God called him to follow, and God escorted him out of his comfort zone and surrounded him with his presence. God's intention was to be in the midst of his people, the Israelites, so they could be light to the rest of the world. God's agenda was to disciple the nation Israel in order for them to disciple the gentiles in manifesting the presence of God.

In the New Testament, Jesus was the master disciple maker and the early church was a disciple-making church. The early church followed what Christ had done during his earthly ministry. The apostles prioritized making disciples through teaching and creating kingdom communities. Luke notes Paul's emphasis on discipleship and writes,

> When they had preached the gospel to that city and had made many disciples, they returned to Lystra and to Iconium and to Antioch, strengthening the souls of the disciples, encouraging them to continue in the faith, and saying that through many tribulations we must enter the kingdom of God. And when they had appointed elders for them in every church, with prayer and

fasting they committed them to the Lord in whom they had believed. (Acts 13:21–23)

We can clearly see the strategy of Paul in the ministry of the gospel: first preaching the gospel followed by making disciples. After encouraging and teaching disciples, they appointed leaders for the churches and committed them to the Lord. Discipleship is how we prepare the church to face challenges. To face the strong opposition from the world, believers have to follow Christ closely. Leaders have to be appointed from disciples who are already proven in following Christ. Christ-led people are capable of leading others to Christ.

When the early church moved from being a movement to being a structured hierarchical organization with the conversion of Constantine in the fourth century, things changed. The focus of the church shifted from making disciples of the nations to a kind of evangelism that was structurally based and government sponsored. As a result, some concerned believers withdrew from the world and the secularized church to monasticism where they continued to disciple believers in small communities.

Christendom became more concerned with the number of converts than with discipling the converts. Contrary to the practice of the early church, the institutional church appointed many leaders who were not disciples but people who were hungry for power and position. Spiritual decline in the churches and the resulting apathy made many people search for alternatives ways of disciple making. Those who saw where the church was heading began to isolate themselves to create a new community that provided discipleship and preserved the spiritual fervor of the church. One of these discipleship strategies was the monastic movement.

> The monastic movements (Celtic, Nestorian, and Benedictine) provided a solid mooring for Christian mission and Christian discipleship in these early centuries of Christian development outside of the Roman world. They preserved learning, secular and spiritual, while promoting political and technological developments that deeply impacted their respective societies.[1]

Monastic movements are sometimes seen as an attempt to isolate believers from the influence of the world, but this is a mistaken view. Monastic movements served the church not only to preserve them from external influence but also helped believers to be focused and transformed in order to do mission. In the

---

1. Stier and Poor, *His Kingdom Come*, 98.

sixteenth century, the Western church hit bottom in spiritual things. It was the lowest moment of discipleship. Here is how Stier and Poor describe the context:

> All over Europe people were turning away, disgusted by the corruption and hypocrisy. The church was literally selling salvation, as people had to pay large amounts of cash to be sure of escaping Hell. In Geneva, the priests were not only immoral themselves, but were also running houses of prostitution. In losing its purity, the church lost its power, and so squandered its authority and its leadership.[2]

Contrary to its divine calling, the church became a stumbling-block to those who were seeking for the truth of the gospel. The corrupt church turned into a business venue for corrupt leaders and the church died spiritually. No discipleship meant no leadership and no leadership meant no church. It was in such a chaotic time that Martin Luther came on the scene with other concerned believers and leaders of the church to lead the Reformation. In fact, the Reformation restored some of the discipleship aspects that had been lost in the structure of the church, but restoring the church to its original movement-based discipleship continued to be a challenge. The Reformers believed and taught the doctrine of the priesthood of all believers and focused on Scripture to equip believers. Both Luther and Calvin not only had disciples but they also worked for the formation of Scripture-based communities.

In the modern church, different groups and individuals have responded to the spiritual decay of the church and society in reviving believers and forming communities that focus on discipleship movements and spiritual reformation. Movements like Methodism, the Salvation Army, the Navigators, Campus Crusade for Christ, and InterVarsity Christian Fellowship are all part of the process of reviving the church and refocusing on discipleship. The church was supposed to implement discipleship because discipleship is a central purpose for the existence of the church. The church is called to proclaim the message of the gospel and make disciples of every nation. The movements awakened the churches to revisit their focus and their approach to mission. Out of these movements came missionaries of the nineteenth and twentieth centuries who were passionate about the conversion of the non-Western world.

The approach used by these missionaries was not discipleship-based evangelism. Influenced by their contemporary context, intentionally or unintentionally, the target of the missionaries was to make converts and civilize

---

2. Ibid., 104.

the cultures of the people they were evangelizing. Their desire was to produce a civilized and educated person through training in schools and churches. Sunquist notes:

> Missionaries saw themselves as helping lower civilizations rise to become more civilized like them. The missionary calling was confused with the civilizing effort of Western nations. Jesus' mission was to make people like Jesus; civilizing meant to make people like us.[3]

In this process of civilization, the cultures of the indigenous peoples were ignored. This practice made Christianity a foreign religion. The divine gospel was overshadowed by human efforts to change the externals rather than to transform the inner person. Related to this, the ambiguity in the relationship between the missionaries and the indigenous people was not conducive to discipleship. Discipleship requires a genuine close relationship that goes beyond the teacher-student relationship. Missionaries were helpful in sharing their knowledge, material blessings and the message of the gospel, but they generally failed to share their own lives and homes with the people they served. They lived in gated buildings with closed doors. They were respected for being good teachers and preachers but not friends. "You have given your goods to feed the poor. You have given your bodies to be burned. We also ask for love. Give us FRIENDS."[4] The sacrifice of missionaries lacked one key aspect of Christianity: friendship that is the base of discipleship. The distance between the missionaries and their converts was a hindrance to discipleship. Most of the missionaries from the West stayed in their own cultural mindset and living style without integrating themselves into the communal culture of the non-Western people. Lack of intimate friendship with the local people kept the influence of missionaries at bay. In the non-Western context, sharing of knowledge has to be joined with sharing lives and resources. This missionary method lacked an appropriate discipleship strategy, and so it minimized the impact of the gospel on the lives of believers.

---

3. Sunquist, *Unexpected*, 13.

4. Scott Sunquist in his book, *The Unexpected Christian Century,* mentions a speech made by Samuel Azariah, Bishop of the Anglican church in South India that reflects the cry of the many non-western churches as they yearn to be disciples not just instructed and parented.

Discipleship – the Meaning

In the contemporary church it is common to hear about discipleship programs and activities. The denominations have various philosophies and approaches to discipleship. For some it is a program for new converts and for others it is a short period of training for members. In some contexts, it varies depending on the priorities and interests of the leader of the program. In order to have a solid strategy for discipleship, churches have to have a biblical foundation, otherwise it is left to the individual leader's desire and opinion. It is important to have a fresh biblical understanding of discipleship in the contemporary global churches.

The Greek word *mathētēs* was in use prior to the New Testament. In its early usage philosophers like Socrates used it to mean a learner with passion and commitment. Unlike the education system today, in the Greco-Roman world students sat at the master's feet, formally and informally studying life-based, well-rounded education.[5] The education system was practical and based on life skills rather than information sharing. It was a continuous commitment to be with the master, learning from him and serving him for a long term. Jesus used a contextually appropriate term and system as he called his disciples to dependency, commitment and relationship that required their whole life. According to M. Wilkins, the term progressed in its meaning from just a learner to an adherent with commitment and devotion. He writes,

> A disciple was one who made a life commitment to a particular master and his way of life. The type of "disciple" and the correspondent life of "discipleship" was determined by the type of master, but commitment to the master and his ways was central.[6]

The meaning of the word progressed from imparting knowledge and skills to becoming connected to the master in a learning relationship that involved a life commitment.

Discipleship has been part of the ministry of the church from its birth. The early church is known for its disciple-making adventure. The approach to discipleship was holistic and comprehensive. Through teaching, rituals, and organizing the saved community, the early church was actively involved in making disciples. On the basis of the teaching of Jesus and the practice of the

---

5. Collinson (*Making Disciples*, 12) in her book discusses the use of the word prior to the NT period. She reports that the term *mathētēs* was first used by Herodotus in the fifth century BCE and appears frequently in classical Greek.

6. Wilkins, *Discipleship*, 39.

early church, Wilkins defines discipleship thus: "Discipleship and discipling imply the process of becoming like Jesus Christ . . . living a fully human life in this world in union with Jesus Christ and growing in conformity in his image."[7] Discipleship has two core foundations, namely, strong attachment to Christ and living a life that demonstrates Christ. It is a meaningful relationship with Christ and becoming a witness for him to the world. It is through the strong attachment with Christ that the believer gets empowered for holy living and witness to others. This commitment to Christ has to be intentional, as Collinson writes:

> Discipleship is an intentional, largely informal, learning activity in which two or a small group of individuals, typically in a community holding to the same religious beliefs, make a voluntary commitment to each other to form a close, personal relationship for an extended period of time, to enable the disciples to learn from the other.[8]

This definition highlights intentionality, informality, community, willingness to learn and extended relationship to accomplish the growth of a believer to the likeness of Christ. I would summarize discipleship as a personal and communal journey towards a transformed, Christ-like life. It is an internal, personal and holistic change in words and actions that spills out to the wider community to reflect Christ to the unreached world. It begins with conversion, which enables the individual or the group to join the community of disciples as they continue to worship God, grow to maturity in Christ, and witness to the world. Discipleship is a comprehensive effort to transform our minds, our ethics and morals, and our social and political judgments, all in order to advance the kingdom of God. The current approaches to discipleship in relation to the ministry of the church can be summarized as follows.

First, discipleship as an effective educational method for the church. For many churches discipleship is a spiritual training method where converts get doctrinal training. According to Collinson, discipleship is a contextual educational system used in the West Asian culture, practiced in both Old and New Testaments, including Jesus and the early church. It was a system suitable to teach religious ideas, beliefs and values. Comparing the discipleship system with the schooling model in today's community, Collinson writes,

---

7. Wilkins, *Discipleship*, 41–42.
8. Collinson, *Making Disciples*, 13.

The discipling model had a capacity encompassing a wide variety of people from different ethnic, cultural, and educational backgrounds. It was not confined by building curriculum or a specific method of teaching. It was ideally suited to the rapidly changing experience of these early communities.[9]

In oral and written cultures, and among literate and illiterate communities, discipleship is an adoptable system. Discipleship as an educational methodology is more than teaching; it is a holistic approach to training.

Second, for some, discipleship is a ministry model. Discipleship as a basic ministry model of the church produces kingdom people. It is not just an education system. It is the calling of the church, the sum total of what the church is called to do. Chris Shirley calls this approach an integrative model; she explains:

In this model, discipleship is not just one component of the church, but a guiding value that permeates every ministry area. The model begins by envisioning a biblical paradigm for the result of the process that answers the question, "Who is a disciple?" . . . "What is discipleship?" . . . "How do we make disciples?" When these three elements are merged, both philosophically and pragmatically, the result should be transformed disciples and healthy churches.[10]

Discipleship is not just a department among other offices of the church but it is a framework and a philosophy for all other ministries. Whatever we do in the four corners of the church building or outside the building towards unreached people has to be framed by our discipleship strategy. Every ministry of the church and every department of a Christian institution should target discipleship as its final goal. This model sees discipleship as the foundation of every ministry in the church. West and Noel categorized literature on models of discipleship in four stages as follows:

These patterns are organized and grouped into four descriptive stages: evangelizing, encouraging, equipping, and empowering. These stages are then compared to the Situational Leadership model as a theoretical framework for understanding the leader-follower dynamic of the discipleship process.[11]

---

9. Ibid., 119.
10. Shirley, "Takes a Church," 208.
11. West and Noel, "Situational Discipleship," 126.

A leader as a disciple maker walks a believer through those four stages. The leader points to Christ and shapes lives after Christ. Every activity in the church has to be geared towards maturing the believers in their faith in Christ. This model takes discipleship as a process of knowing the Word and the world in order to function as an agent of transformation. One of the advocates of this perspective, Charles Dunahoo, writes:

> [This approach] is informational, formational and transformational! Not until we reach the transformational stage will we be discipled in the biblical sense of being transformed into a new person by changing the way we think, bringing every thought into captivity to obeying Christ . . . and not copying the behavior and custom of this world.[12]

Discipleship is perceived as a ministry model that takes a convert from the informational to the transformational stage, molding the individual to become a disciple of Christ. This is not an easy sequence but it is a dynamic process that involves integration and reintegration of ideas and practices.

Third, similar to the above model, scholars like Houston, McCallum and Lowery, and Dodson think of discipleship as a strategy for mentoring and developing leaders and equipping believers for mission.[13] Through intentional relationship and serving one another, believers not only mentor each other but also motivate one another for mission. The right atmosphere to develop leaders and to identify their gifts is a discipleship setting. In a small mentoring group, leaders can mentor other leaders and help them to exercise their gifts, delegating them to different positions. The current leadership crisis demonstrates a divorce between the spiritual gifts of the leader and the moral life of the leader. A person who displays a tremendous gift of leadership often fails to live what he represents. The problem lies in our system of leadership training, which focuses more on intellectual skill training than on holistic life-based mentoring.

Finally, discipleship is a community-building strategy, an embodiment of Christ and an expression of theology. Discipleship is a communal journey. Whether it is an educational method, a ministry model or a way of mentoring others, all of those can only be accomplished in community. New converts need to be embraced by a community that will train them in their new journey. This

---

12. Dunahoo, *Making Kingdom Disciples*, 11.
13. Houston, *Disciples*; McCallum and Lowry, *Organic Discipleship*; Dodson, *Gospel.*

model sees discipleship as a foundation for community building. Community is fundamental in the Christian experience. Edgemon writes,

> Salvation is personal but never private. It affects other persons and carries responsibility. A new Christian is to be nurtured to Christian maturity in the church, drawing strength from other believers, as well as contributing to the growth of others. The church is to be a fellowship wherein members grow through loving relationships, mutual encouragements, and edification, and where they find motivation and spiritual energies for daily living.[14]

Discipleship happens in an intentional fellowship of believers whose community is designed to nurture new converts, to shape their divine identity and mold them to the likeness of Christ. Discipleship is not about producing individual spiritual stars but it is about a community of sojourners dedicated to demonstrating the kingdom of God on earth. Dietrich Bonhoeffer, a German Lutheran minister, rightly understood the role of community in making disciples. He wrote,

> This question of discipleship will be understood in four movements: the foundation of discipleship is the revelation of God in Jesus Christ; the reality of discipleship is the nature of the church – Christ existing as church-community; the action of discipleship is Christopraxis; and the possibility of discipleship is religionless Christianity, which compels the ongoing mission of God in a world come of age.[15]

For Bonhoeffer discipleship is community based on Christ and exists to proclaim and demonstrate the life of Christ as a movement not just as a lifeless ritual. Believers are not gathered to observe rituals and traditions; they are community disciples active in doing God's will. Discipleship as a dynamic community in action to advance the kingdom of God is what Bonhoeffer perceived despite the struggle in the church in his time. The phrase "Christ exists as church-community" says it all. It is the identity of the church and it is how Christ reveals himself in the world. This understanding of discipleship respects the priesthood of all believers and rejects the current celebrity mentality of contemporary believers. If Christianity is to make a positive influence on the community and win lives for Christ, it is important for the

---

14. Edgemon, "Evangelism," 541.
15. Bonhoeffer, *Discipleship*, 226.

church to organize itself as a discipleship community committed to spiritual growth in Christ and to spreading the good news to all the nations.

Discipleship brings people to a genuine and open relationship where they get connected in order to encourage one another in proclaiming the message of the gospel. Believing, growing and working towards the same goal makes discipleship a strong community. Without this close family relationship, it is difficult to bring about the desired maximum impact on the individual convert. Collinson writes this about a discipleship situation:

> Learning relationships involved close, personal, family-like commitment . . . It usually entailed communal living. Learners observed and imitated their teachers as they pursued their daily occupation and assisted them in performing their duties . . . Together they believed in and worked towards common goals.[16]

The relationship in discipleship is learning- and goal-oriented. It is founded on Christ and every believer is connected to grow and mature in the journey as the Spirit of God works through the community. In short, discipleship is an educational strategy, a foundation for the ministries of the church, for leadership development and for genuine community building.

Who Is a Disciple?

Believers are often classified as "born again," "nominal," "disciples," or "Christians," but such a classification is not biblical. Every believer is called to be a disciple. In some denominations, believers are judged by their involvement in the church. For others it is how much money they give to the church that determines their true commitment to their faith. For charismatic believers, it is the manifestation of the spiritual gifts that make a believer a true follower. Then the question is: who is a true disciple according to Scripture? First, a disciple is an individual who has heard the gospel of Jesus Christ and accepted Christ as his/her personal savior. In other words, a disciple is a convert. When Christ approached his disciples, during his earthly ministry, he asked them, "What are you seeking?" (John 1:38) in order to make sure that they were coming with right motives. A disciple is not a perfect person but it is someone who is willing to grow in Christ. Second, a disciple is a committed follower of Christ.

---

16. Collinson, *Making Disciples*, 23.

A disciple is one who has understood the cost of discipleship and is willing to pay the price. Here is how Christ described the commitment of discipleship:

> And calling the crowd to him with his disciples, he said to them, "If anyone would come after me, let him deny himself and take up his cross and follow me. For whoever would save his life will lose it, but whoever loses his life for my sake and the gospel's will save it." (Mark 8:34–35)

Christ was clearly communicating that the life of a disciple is a life that involves self-denial. It is a sacrificial life of carrying the cross of Christ. A disciple's commitment to Christ takes precedent over all other commitments in their life. All four Gospels reiterate the same concept of discipleship, as Samra writes:

> Therefore, in the Gospels discipleship (the process of becoming like Christ) was accomplished by being physically with Christ, seeing what He did, hearing what He said, being corrected by Him, and following His example. That a disciple is to learn to follow Christ in humility, self-sacrifice, and unconditional love is presented in Mark 10:35–44, Luke 10:25–37, and John 13:1–17, and is modeled in His death. Jesus taught that a disciple must be fully committed to God. (Matt 6:24; 8:18–22)[17]

Of course, today Christ is not present physically with believers but is with them through his Spirit. A disciple has to be sensitive to listen to the Spirit of God and be conscious of God's presence in his/her daily life. A disciple is an individual who has made a full commitment to follow Christ and is fully surrendered to Christ.

Third, a disciple lives and proclaims the kingdom of God. Jesus's disciples had an agenda and purpose for their lives: spreading the message of the kingdom. The primary teaching of Christ to his disciples and to the wider audience was the presence of the kingdom in their midst. Prior to Christ's birth, John the Baptist urged repentance in preparation for the kingdom of God and Jesus continued proclaiming the imminence of the kingdom. According to De Ridder, the criticisms of Jesus from both the disciples and the leaders of the time were related to the kingdom of God. He writes,

> . . . whereas he (Jesus) criticized the Twelve for putting themselves before the kingdom, Jesus criticized the opponents for putting their religion before the kingdom of God. They put tradition of

---

17. Samra, "Biblical View," 226.

the elders before the justice and mercy of God (Mark 7:3); they put ritual legalism before their concern for men; they put external purity before their own inner righteousness.[18]

It is intriguing to ask what Christ would criticize if he were to visit our contemporary churches. Just like some of the people in Jesus's day, the current global church is putting material things, race and power before the kingdom of God. The attitude and the actions of a disciple should be focused on the kingdom; they should reflect the kingdom, and proclaim the kingdom. The identity of a disciple should be drawn from Christ, not from earthly possessions, ethnic background or religious affiliation. A disciple is an individual who has turned away from his/her sin and has started the journey to Christ in a community of believers, committed to follow Christ and to proclaim his kingdom. A disciple is an individual sold-out for the cause of Christ and for the coming of his kingdom.

Making Disciples

There are multiple reasons why we should take discipleship seriously. It benefits the church community and it brings a perfect unity among the believers. It is what Christ has commanded the church to do and what he demonstrated during his earthly ministry. It is the best strategy to mature the church and equip it for mission.

Commanded by Christ

Christ commanded his disciples to make other disciples, and he promised his eternal presence with them. Discipleship is not an afterthought designed by the early church, rather it is a command given by Christ and contextually applied in the early church. Though the Great Commission is written at the end of the Gospels, the discipleship issue was at the center of Christ's ministry and teaching throughout his time on earth. The Great Commission is what Christ has in mind and what he has demonstrated and what he has commanded the church. It is the grand total of what the gospel writers were communicating. Mortimer Arias writes,

---

18. De Ridder, *Discipling the Nations*, 138.

So, if we are serious about understanding Matthew's version of the commission, read it in the context of that gospel. Viewed in context, the "Great Commission" is the climax of Matthew's Gospel, "the summary," and "the key to the understanding of the whole Gospel." In other words, to understand the Gospel of Matthew we must decipher this "last commission," and, conversely, to understand the "last commission" we must comprehend the totality of Matthew.[19]

It is a grand command with the greatest promise. Jesus promised to be with the church as the church seeks to obey him in proclaiming the message to make disciples of all nations. What matters for Jesus is not the elegance of the church's structure or the beauty of the building, but it is making disciples in every context! More than the programs and politics that the contemporary church is entangled with, what Christ has commanded then and today is to make faithful followers for him.

Some missionaries are driven by the harvest metaphor and so will move from resistant places to places where the harvest is ready, or give priority to receptive places. It is true that some places are ready to receive missionaries and their message, while other places are resistant and violent. In such cases, we have to ask critical questions about the reasons for such receptivity and resistance. We should dig deeper to understand the issues the people are dealing with rather than rushing to the so-called receptive places. In addition, if the people are receptive we should make sure that we train them to be disciples not just converts. We should target holistic transformation. That does not mean we have to care less for the suffering world, but it is better to work towards a complete transformation than to travel only half the journey. Bruce Ashford writes,

> In an effort to reach the lost and dying as quickly as possible, some missionaries have embraced a streamlined missiological strategy that seeks to proclaim the gospel, form the new groups into churches, and then move on. The motivation is understandable given the great need of so many lost souls and so few workers, but the result of this philosophy is devastating.[20]

---

19. Arias, "Church," 410.
20. Ashford, *Theology*, 188.

It is very important to have a balanced approach to our mission and evangelism. Our evangelism is incomplete if we fail to make disciples out of the converts. Through the work of the Holy Spirit, people make decisions to follow Christ but then it is the task of the community to train and model the Christian life. Ashford adds,

> The task of reaching the unreached is necessary and biblical, but it is simply the first step in our obedience to Christ's Great Commission among the people where we serve. Jesus did not send us to "get decisions from all men" but rather to "make disciples of all nations."[21]

The motivation to spread the gospel as quickly as possible without it taking root in the hearts of people is not what Christ designed. To reiterate the point, the calling of the church is not to gather converts and brag about how many registered members we have in the churches but to make disciples who are citizens of the heavenly kingdom of God.

Modeled by Christ

During his few years on earth, Christ's focus was making disciples and equipping them for the work ahead. The mission of the disciples was to continue the work that had been started by Jesus. According to Andreas Köstenberger,

> The Fourth Gospel describes the mission of the disciples in terms of "harvesting" (4:38), "fruitbearing" (15:8, 16) and "witnessing" (15:27). All of these terms place the disciples in the humble position of extending the mission of Jesus.[22]

The agenda is set by Christ and he demonstrated how to accomplish it. Despite the busy schedule and service to the needs of people around, Jesus intentionally targeted the Twelve and taught them both formally and informally, in both theory and practice. He used stories and parables to teach in open-air meetings and in small house gatherings. The Gospels describe how Christ trained his disciples and taught them continuously as they struggled to understand the concept of being disciples of Christ. Three key aspects of discipleship are worth highlighting here: it was an intentional relationship, not accidental; it was a

---

21. Ibid., 190.
22. Köstenberger, "Review of *The Discipleship Paradigm*," 141.

voluntary commitment, not imposed; and it was a learning community where disciples learned from Jesus and from each other.

Jesus in his discipleship process selected people and called them "to be with him, and to be sent out to proclaim the message, and to have authority to cast out demons" (Mark 3:14–15). The disciples in turn responded to his call, followed him willingly and learned from him. Jesus was not manipulative in his relationship; he gave them freedom to leave if they wanted. Christ formed a small community of faithful individuals who had a close personal relationship with him and were determined to learn from him.

We can learn from the training methods of Jesus. First, the discipleship process was multidimensional. It was designed to address the different needs of the disciples. He taught with parables and metaphors in ways that enabled them to capture the concepts. He also demonstrated his teachings in real-life situations where they could taste and see what it meant to follow him. In addition, Jesus encouraged them to reflect on his actions as they did, for example, after he washed their feet (John 13:12). Jesus spoke to his disciples individually, in small groups and also in larger crowds. The contemporary way to put it would be to say that he preached big crusades, he gave leadership training, taught discipleship classes and visited families in need.

Second, Jesus's discipleship methodology was relational. He loved his disciples (John 13), he prayed for them (John 17), and he was patient with them as they struggled to understand the kingdom concept. They were not the smartest of the community, but after spending quality time with Jesus they became passionate about the gospel and ready to make a difference. Samra writes,

> Jesus also encouraged the Twelve to attempt various things themselves. If they failed, He corrected them, and when they were successful, He rejoiced. Examples of such activities include Peter's attempt to walk on water (Matt 14:28–31), the failure of the disciples to cast out a demon (Luke 9:37–45), and the evangelistic missions of the Twelve and the Seventy (9:1–6; 10:1–20).[23]

Christ could have spent his time differently than investing in a few disciples. He could have built a big cathedral for generations to visit as a historical icon or he could have recruited a huge army to conquer and subdue his enemies. But he chose to disciple a few people to be with him and follow him in advancing the kingdom of God. His wise investment in the lives of disciples paid off when

---

23. Samra, "Biblical View," 234.

the apostles went out to preach the gospel to the ends of the earth filled by the Holy Spirit. Jesus came to save humanity and invest in humanity.

Following in Christ's footsteps, the church should not prioritize institutions, programs or organizations before discipleship. "Jesus' followers are called to imitate Jesus' selfless devotion in seeking his sender's glory, to submit to their sender's will, and to represent their sender accurately and know him intimately."[24] That is the call of all disciples of every generation. True Christianity puts Christ at the center. It is all about obeying his will and representing him on earth. The Christian life begins with accepting God's grace through Christ, continues with following Christ in expanding his kingdom and consummates with his second coming as all the believers gather to worship God for ever and ever.

Discipleship: Backbone to Mission

The Great Commission text of Matthew's Gospel (Matt 28:19–20) is one of the most preached sermons in mission conferences, commissioning of missionaries and in fundraising for overseas missions. It is always proof-texted to argue for sending missionaries. It also serves as a motivational text for going overseas to preach the good news of Christ. William Carey, Donald McGavran and other advocates of mission have argued from this text to convince believers to do mission. After many debates and discussions, there is now a strong consensus among scholars that Matthew's Gospel is focused on missional discipleship.[25] Bosch writes, "Today scholars agree that the entire Gospel points to these final verses: all the threads woven into the fabric of Matthew, from chapter 1 onwards, draw together here."[26] According to Bosch, mission in Matthew is more than just spreading the word. It is teaching, equipping and maturing believers to fit into the kingdom of God. It is Matthew's purpose in writing the gospel to emphasize and remind the community of believers about their calling and mission: to make disciples. Mission has to be backed by a strong community of disciples who know their calling and commission.

Reports of many missionaries indicate the number of converts, which generates excitement and funding, but a discipling process is more difficult to report. The reality in the history of missions is that the emphasis on going and

---

24. Köstenberger, "Review of *The Discipleship Paradigm*," 217.

25. Arias, "Church"; Bosch, *Transforming Mission*; and Chris Wright, *Mission of God*, goes further to argue that the entire Bible is a missionary book.

26. Bosch, *Transforming Mission*, 57.

converting has taken precedence over teaching and discipling. In critiquing such an approach Bosch writes,

> The Matthean Jesus sounds extremely didactic and legalistic and is an embarrassment, particularly for Protestants who would prefer to hear about proclamation rather than teaching, about forgiveness of sins and the power of the Holy Spirit rather than keeping commandments.[27]

The pressure for quick success in evangelism and its measurement in terms of just numbers of converts has put discipleship out of sight in the mission of the church.

But Matthew in his gospel urges the believing community to teach the converts to keep the commandments given by Christ. Matthew encourages action and visible fruits of conversion in a believer – things that can function as salt and light to the world. Bosch notes that the phrase "teaching them to observe all that I have commanded you" (Matt 28:19) refers back to the first of these discourses, the sermon on the mount.[28] Mission is more than preaching the words and converting people to the kingdom of God; it is making people committed followers of Christ and makers of disciples. Mission without discipleship would appear to be like a body without a soul. Discipleship is the backbone to mission. The gospel of Jesus Christ is not just information to pass on; it is the power of God to transform individual lives and communities. The transformation can only happen when we train believers to be disciples of Christ.

Mission as Imitating Christ in Discipleship

Michael Wilkins, in his thorough discussion of the use of the term *mathētēs* in Matthew's Gospel, concludes that the unique use of different terms related to discipleship in Matthew encourages the contemporary church to contextualize the concept. In his words, "Matthew has created a literary device to show the way Jesus taught his disciples and to show how that teaching can relate to his church."[29] Matthew wanted his community to take a lesson for their own contemporary context in which they could practice being disciples and discipling others. Wilkins argues that what Christ did with his disciples is not

27. Ibid., 24.
28. Ibid., 69.
29. Wilkins, *Discipleship*, 171.

just a story for study or meditation; it is a lesson from which a church can learn about success and failure in being disciples and making disciples. He contends,

> The disciples are positive examples of what Matthew expects from his church, a negative example of warning, and a mixed group who are able to overcome their lack through the teaching of Jesus. The historical disciples become a means of encouragement, warning, and instruction as examples.[30]

The teaching and practice of Jesus is expected to be contextualized in our specific contexts. Wilkins' argument makes sense when we think of Matthew's community as it originated in Judaism; nonetheless by the time of the composition of the gospel the community functioned outside the confines of its original *locus operandi*.[31] In the early formation of the Christian communities, Matthew wanted the believers to understand their identity as followers of Christ. He laid a foundation for the universal church to know its calling and purpose of existence – that is, disciple making. An important section of Matthew's Gospel, the sermon on the mountain, contains materials Jesus used to train the disciples how to live the life of the kingdom, as they became missionaries in their own contexts.

It was also timely and appropriate for Matthew to present discipleship as a reconciliatory movement. In a context where the Jews had many reasons to hate the gentiles, Matthew is teaching that disciples of Christ must always share the message of reconciliation despite their cultural differences.

> Whenever we date Matthew's Gospel, then, he addressed an audience that had suffered at the hands of Gentiles and may have felt every reason to hate them. Yet Matthew's message summons them to cross all barriers to reach these very Gentiles who had been their enemies – even Canaanites and Roman officers. If Matthew could summon his first audience to sacrifice their own prejudice in such a way, his Gospel summons us to do no less. He summons us to surmount ethnic and cultural prejudice, to love and to serve others no matter what the cost. This is a message of ethnic reconciliation in Christ as well as a summons to global mission.[32]

---

30. Ibid., 172.

31. Foster, *Community*, 20.

32. Keener, "Matthew's Missiology," 3.

In this discipleship journey, the members grow into an ideal community, avoiding all the racial and ethnic tensions in demonstrating a unity that surpasses all human efforts. One of the challenges of Christianity in today's world is racism and ethnocentrism. The issue of race is everywhere: in politics, in sport, in business and even in the church. To counter this challenge, the church has to produce disciples who are transformed by the gospel and are ready to transform their world. So far, I have discussed the need for contextualized discipleship and the biblical foundation of discipleship. If discipleship is biblical, then how should the church in every context effectively establish contextualized discipleship? This is an area where research is needed. Though the Scripture gives us Jesus's model of discipleship in the first century, how can we apply it to our own specific contexts? We need understanding of the key biblical principles and contextual issues in order to integrate them into our approach to contextualized discipleship. If the church of Christ is to grow towards the likeness of Christ, three key areas of the spiritual journey of a believer have to be integrated. These key aspects are: (1) the believer's conversion, a new birth and a spiritual beginning, (2) rituals, the believer's practical experience that intensifies and brings fresh memories, and (3) the formation of a community that solidifies the believer's thoughts and experiences and develops a culture of discipleship for generations to come. These three aspects are discussed in the next chapter.

3

Integrating Conversion, Rituals and Community

The main issue with discipleship in contemporary churches is not that it does not exist, but that it is not contextualized and organized. Every church has a discipleship program, among other programs, that runs for a limited period of time. The question is: Do churches have an effective discipleship approach? And how is discipleship contextualized? In many churches discipleship is a program for new converts that is classroom-based and cognitively focused. A convert in their first four to six months gets religious instruction in a lecture format until the day of baptism. At the end of the instruction before baptism, usually there is some sort of evaluation – an oral interview or a written exam. After baptism, the convert becomes a member of the church and gets involved in adult Sunday school or small groups or both. Such a training system has some defects.

To begin with, it is an educational curriculum based on intellectual understanding. It is mainly information sharing that neglects the other aspects of human nature. One can easily get away with putting on a mask during the instruction hours and continuing to live a double life. In societies where oral communication is the main cultural way of training it would be difficult to bring a significant life change with cognitive-based teaching. A more comprehensive and practical approach would address such contexts as the people often deal with – multidimensional problems that are practical, relational and social in nature. For instance, if a convert hears a lecture on the Trinity in the classroom, they would wonder how that would relate to their being a good husband or wife. The cognitive approach can help people to have the right information, but people need the right skills to translate the concept into action. As a result, churches can produce intellectual converts with unconverted wills and emotions. The converts can impress their teachers with their knowledge of the Scripture but may disappoint the Lord in their unchanged behaviors or loose relationships.

Moreover, in many churches the teaching materials for discipleship are not contextually prepared. In many cases they are copied from other contexts and lack relevance in the given context. Some use translated materials that lack attention to local issues and fail to facilitate the believers' growth in their social context. For instance, some Western discipleship materials include a topic on the existence of God. In Africa, where the existence of God is generally agreed upon, it is irrelevant to discuss such a topic; instead the issue should be, how can one relate to God? The evaluation of the spiritual life of the converts is often based on the culture of the missionaries or the evangelists rather than on Scripture and the existing cultural context.

Converts are judged by their classroom performance or involvement. The evaluation system is neither comprehensive nor biblical. Some extroverts can easily convince the leaders that they are mature believers by their external performance, and introverts can be mistakenly judged as immature. Converts who have misunderstood the gospel and have been converted to something other than Christ can turn out to be the worst enemies of the gospel. They can distort the image of Christianity and put an obstacle before the watching world. Discipleship has to be contextualized at every step of the believers' spiritual journey as they engage with their culture.

Contextualization and Discipleship

Contextualization is an attempt to bridge the gap between the message of the gospel and the culture of the people. It is the believing community's continual dialogue with Scripture and their changing context. Discipleship is a process of maturing believers so that they can engage with the context properly and make other disciples of Christ. People live in a specific context and their lives are shaped by the context they live in. It is difficult to understand people without understanding their context. It is difficult to discuss one without the other.

Contextualization and discipleship are two sides of one coin. Both work on the spiritual growth of believers and their effective witness to their world. Contextualization equips believers to understand their context and the text of Scripture in its original context in order to communicate the eternal message to the existing contemporary culture. Teresa Chai mentions three concerns that contextualization raises:

The first concern is that missionaries tend to introduce their cultural heritage as an integral part of the gospel . . . The second concern is the necessity of putting the gospel into the new context so that the gospel and the resulting church will not seem foreign in its new setting. The third concern is that converts may include elements of their culture, which alters or eliminates aspects of the gospel upon which the integrity of the gospel depends.[1]

Contextualization serves as a facilitator between gospel and culture and protects the gospel from syncretism by both the missionary and indigenous cultures. The key components of the journey of a disciple include understanding the gospel and making Christ the center of one's life. Contextualization and discipleship work towards the transformation of the individual believer in displaying Christ's likeness in his/her everyday life. Therefore, a mature believer or faithful disciple of Christ is an agent of contextualization as he/she continuously engage with the context. In the process of contextualization, the believer becomes more mature than before.

The concept of contextualization came onto the scene in the 1970s, a time when culture was demonized in Africa and the social context in Latin America had been ignored by the earlier missionaries and first-generation Christians. Since that time, contextualization has been applied to ideas, cultures, worldviews and rituals in specific contexts in order to serve the communication of the gospel. The concept has helped missionaries and indigenous believers to deal with cultures and integrate the positive aspects into their Christianity.

At the beginning stages, contextualization was concerned with the appropriate communication of the gospel for reaching the unreached, because the earlier missiologists focused on the shortcoming of the missionaries in their communication endeavor and its impact on the local believers.[2] It is true that communicating the gospel is the core component of mission, but there is much to be done even after the individual is converted to Christianity. Focus on communication of the message made contextualization less comprehensive, but missiologists later corrected the approach.

Of course, some evangelicals had reservations: contextualization could possibly promote context over the eternal message. Part of the concern of evangelicals with Kraft's approach to contextualization was related to the authority of Scripture. Kraft, who was a professor at Fuller Seminary, believes the

---

1. Chai, "Look at Contextualization," 5.
2. Chang and Morgan, "Paul G. Hiebert," 204.

Bible as a case book of God, which is different from the traditional evangelical view of Scripture. Some evangelicals feared that more focus on culture would mean less focus on Scripture. Kraft's "primary concern was to discover the meaning of equivalence and cross-cultural communication through the use of cultural forms in order to create local contextual understanding."[3] The concern of conservative evangelicals is valid if we do not have disciples who are able to discern the contextual issues through the lens of Scripture. Nominal believers who pursue cultural concerns uncritically might make the church lose its sharp edge and prophetic voice. Though evangelicals were slow to embrace contextualization, the need for a contextual approach is approved by the majority of Christians. However, the type and the level of contextualization is always a matter of debate. Currently we find that the horizon of contextualization has been expanded and scholars have begun to discuss "appropriate Christianity"[4] in a more comprehensive way. Moreau writes,

> The current approach towards contextualization as essentially a theological enterprise is an appropriate foundation, but no more than a foundation. The question we need to address is this, "What type of edifice should we build on the theological foundations that have been developed over the past thirty years of writing on contextualization?" To answer this, I will outline a contextualization paradigm that goes beyond theologizing to include all that the Christian faith is and all that following Christ calls us to do. Such an approach may be called *comprehensive* contextualization.[5]

Comprehensive contextualization is a holistic approach where believers continually engage with their context equipped by the Word of God as they grow towards the likeness of Christ and positively influence their society. How far culture should influence one's spirituality and how far Christianity should transform one's culture is a continual progressive dialogue. For instance, cultural diversity is a blessing, but if cultural identity comes before one's identity in Christ, racism and ethnocentrism can take over in our relationship. On the other hand, if one rejects his/her own cultural identity then identity crisis is imminent. Therefore, a balanced approach that is comprehensive needs to be applied.

---

3. Ibid., 200.

4. Kraft, 2005.

5. Moreau, "Contextualization That Is Comprehensive," 1.

Contextualization in our discipleship is essential in order that the church may become mature and be able to address the critical needs of the people in their contexts. Daniel Shaw writes,

> If the intent of gospel communication is to enable people to become more like God intended them to be, that is, to display God's image, then transformation in those who bring the gospel and in those who hear and "receive" it will move both toward that goal. This understanding has important theological implications for long-established missiological themes surrounding God's will, the incarnation . . . how the message works itself out in a new environment, and how new disciples will themselves be missional.[6]

The goal of contextualization has to go beyond just communicating the gospel to the transformation of the community through an incarnational lifestyle to bring the kingdom of God. The fruit of the contextualized gospel should be faithful disciples of Christ who are equipped not only to reflect theologically in their specific context but also to become effective witnesses to others around.

Contextualization is ultimately about helping believers to become mature and equipping them to be effective witnesses. It is about making disciples of all nations. But contextualization has been thwarted and twisted to serve other purposes. When contextualization is narrowed to just understanding and lifting up culture without exposing it to the eternal Word of God, it can lead to spiritual setback. Let me mention some of the unintended outcomes of the failure to integrate contextualization with discipleship. First, uncritical contextualization can lead to syncretism, and traditional practices can overwhelm Christianity to the extent of watering down the gospel. Many theologians took that path and became advocates of culture at the expense of the gospel. In such instances, the role of the gospel in the community is downplayed. Chitando writes, ". . . [the] God of Christianity is the same as 'the God' [of] the ATRs . . . there is nothing that Christianity can add to ATRs. ATR is 'matching' or even transcending Christianity in some respects."[7] In fact, no culture has a saving power and message like the divine gospel. Culture may have some elements of general revelation but it does not have a salvific potential.

---

6. Shaw, "Beyond Contextualization," 208.

7. Chitando, *Inculturation*, 98. African theologians Samuel G. Kibicho, Gabriel Setiloane and Christian Gaba hold this position that Christianity is a radical continuation of the ATR (African Traditional Religion). Quoted by Ezra Chitando in *Inculturation and Postcolonial Discourse in African Theology,* edited by Edward P. Antonio, 2006.

In response to the missionary approach to culture, many African theologians try to lift culture beyond its limits. Replacing the divine message with culture is not a purpose of contextualization. Rather it is finding the right place and role of culture in understanding the divine message properly. Some theologians, in their search for cultural identity and meaning, rejected the value of the gospel in their lives. Chitando adds, "Fired by cultural nationalism and galvanized by a vision of theological continuity between ATR and Christianity, African Christian theologians have scoured the religious landscape for 'valuables' to carry into Christianity."[8] There is nothing wrong about searching for more meaningful discourse with our culture and tradition, but if it eclipses the message of the Scripture it needs to refocus. Our calling is to be followers of Christ not disciples of our culture. Our values and actions should be Christ-centered rather than culture-biased. Because of what happened in mission history regarding culture and tradition, culture is becoming untouchable these days. Missionaries are becoming too wary of commenting on cultures because of the fear of repercussion. Culture has such a powerful grip on humanity that without a transformed mind it is difficult to analyze and see the hidden ungodly practices of our tradition. The global body of Christ, as diverse as we are, needs to work together in discovering the blind spots in our cultures.

Second, bad contextualization also contributes to the liberal approach to Scripture and to the doctrine of salvation, as the revival of cultures brings with it doubts about the centrality of Christ and the authority of Scripture. Udo Etuk asks, "Why now should we be fed on the history, the folklore, the allegory and poetry of the Hebrews (however beautiful) that had no functional connection with Africa?"[9] Respect for Scripture and its culture dwindles as believers turn to their own contemporary culture and tradition as more relevant and important than salvation through Christ alone.

Third, contextualization is supposed to clarify things and to bring greater understanding to both culture and the gospel, but in some cases when contextualization is poorly done it ends up confusing believers. Udo Etuk writes this about contextualization in Africa: "The difficulty with the theology of contextualization and the call for an African Christian theology is that what emerges is neither Christian nor theological, but a capitulation to traditional cultural practices."[10] In other words, it is confusing to believers who may be

---

8. Ibid.
9. Etuk, "Theology," 218.
10. Ibid., 217.

swayed from rejecting culture to mixing culture with Christianity. Because of such confusion African believers are drawn into new so-called apostolic movements that mainly teach about earthly blessings.

That is not to discredit the progress made through the efforts of contextualization. Since the introduction of contextualization, missionaries are more equipped to understand cultures, and churches are growing by using the contextualized approach in their preaching of the gospel. Despite the progress made there are also areas that need more research and integration to serve the church better. First, there needs to be more integration of theory and practice on the mission field. Theories, models, and theses regarding contextualization have been advanced before being applied in real-life circumstances. Exceptional dissertations and books are written on contextualization, yet the missionaries and practitioners are not connected to the academic research and publication. For example, I wrote my dissertation on "contextualization of the gospel among the nomadic people of southern Ethiopia."[11] I came up with many insightful ideas but the dissertation is shelved in the library and I am busy in teaching at a higher level, and so the evangelists and missionaries on the field benefit nothing from it. Contextualization continues to have many advocates but few practitioners who put the theory into practice.

Second, contextualization needs to incorporate the spiritual and the transformational dimensions. Contextualization is a spiritual ministry. It has to be carried out with much prayer and study of the Word of God as well as of the cultural context. A community of disciples has to conduct the process in a way that facilitates their growth as a community and advances the kingdom of God. If contextualization is just an academic exercise, and mere human effort divorced from spiritual exercise, it can't produce disciples. It should always keep the sharp edge of the gospel and the prophetic voice of the church. Contextualizers have to acknowledge their need of the Holy Spirit's help in discerning contextual elements that should be incorporated or rejected. In other words, contextualization should lead to discipleship and disciples should contextualize in order to transform their communities. Effective contextualization requires a transformed mind to come to the right understanding of the gospel and to challenge and transform the existing cultural context in creating a community that is centered in Christ. Indeed, the priority of contextualizing the contextualizer is critical.

---

11. Ermias Mamo, "Knowing God in Ritual Context," 2008.

In order to integrate contextualization and discipleship to equip believers for mission we need to discuss areas of integration. The journey of faith has different stages and those stages need to be understood appropriately to facilitate the process. I will mention three areas of integration. First, discipleship begins with conversion. Understanding conversion, its biblical meaning, and its application in different cultural contexts helps converts to begin their spiritual journey with right motives and a sound foundation. The integrative approach of contextualization and discipleship helps to bridge the journey of the convert from a sinful life to a life that reflects Christ and proclaims his kingdom.

Second, the journey of discipleship is strengthened by moments and milestones represented by rituals. These rituals or sacraments add energy to the individuals as they continue the journey with different experiences, both physically and spiritually. All cultures have rituals but the role of rituals may differ from culture to culture. Therefore, contextualizing the sacraments in different cultural contexts and making them available for the benefit of the believers is an issue that requires extensive study and an integrated approach.

Finally, as we have said before, discipleship can take place only in community. The community helps to shape the believer's identity and growth. Without community support, conversion lacks a strong foothold. Moreover, rituals can only become meaningful and efficacious in the presence of community. This is not to underplay the role of the Holy Spirit, as an agent of conversion, in convicting people. Human efforts and methods without the help of the Spirit of God fall short of bringing a life change. Gordon Smith writes,

> The outpouring of the Spirit as described in Acts 2 coincides with the formation of the church; we cannot divorce the work of the Spirit from the formative role of the Christian community. The church, the community of faith, is necessarily the mediator of religious experience. Only the Spirit of God can bring about the spiritual renewal and regeneration that is sought by those coming to faith. But the church is a kind of midwife, a necessary and critical means by which this new birth is experienced.[12]

Figuratively speaking, the midwifery role of the church is important for healthy delivery of the new babies and their spiritual growth to maturity. Conversion, rituals, and community are key ingredients for a successful discipleship journey. If we take discipleship as a spiritual journey, contextualization serves as a street light to shine on the darkest areas of

---

12. Smith, *Beginning Well*, 35.

the road. It is my conviction that these themes are a good example of how contextualization and discipleship can be integrated in order to equip the church for its God-given mission. Of course, these are not the only issues needing integration but they are the most fundamental and core issues that create a framework for other areas. Discipleship without contextualization cannot be effective and contextualization without discipleship will fail to serve the church.

According to the Scripture, we are disciples of Christ on a spiritual journey. Our cultures should serve us in our journey, not hinder us. Contextualized discipleship should lead us to a confidence that though we are from diverse cultures we are growing together in genuine dialogue towards the likeness of Christ. Of course, our history and background play a great role in shaping the way we see and understand things. Nevertheless, as people of God we should have a transformed mind that understands every cultural narrative in relation to the metanarrative given in the Scripture.

Conversion: The Entry Point to the Discipleship Journey

Discipleship is a spiritual journey that begins with conversion. The individual or the group has to decide voluntarily to join the community of Christ in acknowledging the gift of eternal life in Christ Jesus. Conversion involves a positive response to the knocking of the Holy Spirit on our hearts. As Andrew Walls comments,

> Christianity without conversion is no longer Christianity, because conversion means turning to God. It involves forsaking sin, with its self-deifying attitudes and self-serving conduct, and turning to Christ, whose death on the cross is the basis for God's offer of mercy.[13]

Christian conversion is a decision to learn and know about Christ and move away from every other controlling power in our lives. How people begin their spiritual journey is crucial to continuing the journey and finishing it well. Wrong motives or faulty foundations affect the course of the journey. Converts who join the church to please their family and friends will only stay in the church as long as they have good relationships. As Kyle Idleman rightly reminds the church, Jesus is not looking for fans who would wear the t-shirts

---

13. Walls, "The Significance of Global Christianity," 27.

and put stickers on their vehicles; he is looking for disciples who are committed to live a transformed life in the Spirit. He writes,

> It may seem that there are many followers of Jesus, but if they were honestly to define the relationship they have with him I am not sure it would be accurate to describe them as followers. It seems to me that there is a more suitable word to describe them. They are not followers. They are fans of Jesus.[14]

As we know from the sports world, fans mainly cheer or support a certain team or club. Their commitment varies from emotional attachment to financial contribution, but they can switch anytime if the club offends them. They are not expected to be lifetime followers. Similarly, some believers are just fans who cheer the cause of Christianity but have not given their lives to Christ. One New Testament example would be Nicodemus, who had a positive attitude towards Christ but was not sure that he could commit himself to follow Jesus. He came to meet Jesus at night. Nevertheless, in the conversation with Nicodemus, Jesus clearly spelled out the need for conversion. To be a true follower of Christ Nicodemus had to change his status from being fan to being a disciple.

> Truly, truly, I say to you, unless one is born of water and the Spirit, he cannot enter the kingdom of God. That which is born of the flesh is flesh, and that which is born of the Spirit is spirit. Do not marvel that I said to you, "You must be born again." The wind blows where it wishes, and you hear its sound, but you do not know where it comes from or where it goes. So it is with everyone who is born of the Spirit. (John 3:5–8)

These firm words of Christ show that there is no way around the requirement of conversion. The discipleship journey begins with new birth and new life in the family of Christ.

The postmodern liberal culture has influenced the meaning of the word "conversion" if not deleted it from the religious vocabulary. There is compromise on the meaning of conversion and the necessity for it. The global church needs to revisit its conviction about conversion in its contemporary context. To begin with, the global conversion rate is not so great, as David Barrett points out. Though the church in the non-Western world is growing, the global growth rate is stagnant. He writes, "The proportion of Christians will remain stable at an average of 34 percent of the world population, the same percentage as in

---

14. Idleman, *Not a Fan*, 24.

1900."[15] After a century of great missionary work, the gain has balanced the losses and the percentage stays the same. If Barrett is right, the conversion issue should come to the table for discussion on what is happening to the harvest. Why is the global rate of conversion stagnant?

Second, with theological liberalism, the debate on the necessity of conversion shifted the meaning of conversion and its role in the lives of Christians. The age-old theological foundation of salvation only through Christ was questioned. Salvific status was awarded to general revelation in culture, which implies that culture is equal to Scripture. Missionaries were blamed for destroying culture and imposing conversion. As a result, conversion is perceived as an imposition or an expression of political incorrectness. Converts are expected not to cross any spiritual, social and theological boundary, but to add Christian values to their existing beliefs.

The meaning of conversion is modified and adjusted to the concept of the day. According to the social gospel theologians, "salvation is a corporate, not an individual, process. The origin of sin is not rebellion against a holy Creator but social alienation from one another. Sinful acts are those that alienate us from one another . . . they transferred the root of sin from the heart to society."[16] The biblical teaching of conversion as rejecting sin and sinful behavior to follow Christ and his will was reinterpreted as the pursuit of social wellbeing and peaceful existence. Rauschenbusch, following Schleiermacher, advocated the idea of the kingdom of God as a religious ethical condition that is found in the lives of practitioners.[17]

Third, the meaning of conversion lost its global theological consensus and became different things to different people, so that the behavioral mark for a convert is different in different contexts. The line between believers and non-believers has become more blurry. In the past, missionary culture dictated the standard for converts' behavior. Today, it is different. Every culture tries to define conversion in its own ways – what it means and what it entails. But conversion has to be defined according to the Scripture not according to the individual's experience or cultural understanding. Because of such culture-bound understanding, believers from different contexts can sometimes find it difficult to work with one another.

---

15. Barrett, "Annual Statistical Table," 25.

16. Wells, *Turning to God*, 16.

17. Ibid.

Let me illustrate my point. Years ago, I met an American girl who had just come back from a short-term mission trip to Ethiopia. She was a passionate newly converted college student who had an interest in cross-cultural mission. She was disappointed by her experience in Ethiopia and she regretted taking the trip. After arriving in Ethiopia with her friends, she was paired with an Ethiopian female college student to go out and witness in public. The Ethiopian girl saw a tattoo of a snake on the American girl's back that shocked her, and while they were in the taxi she heard her humming a Michael Jackson song – strike two. For Ethiopian Christians, the standard is no secular music and no tattoos, especially of a snake – "no way!" The Ethiopian girl was so troubled with what she saw from her American witnessing mate that she decided to confront her before they witnessed to others. She blurted out with anger, "Are you sure you are a Christian?" That shocked the American girl. From the American girl's perspective, the pride and prejudice reflected in the Ethiopian girl's attitude did not display Christian character. However, before you blame the Ethiopian girl, snakes and signs of snakes are connected automatically to witchdoctors and devil worship in Ethiopia. A snake as a pet is unthinkable for Christians, let alone to have as a tattoo. For the American girl, her tattoo had nothing to do with her spiritual life, or she may have had it before she came to Christ. Different contexts and different standards of conversion and spirituality affect the unity of believers from diverse contexts. Finally, the two girls failed to understand each other and decided to quit their mission. That is why this American girl carried a sore spot from her mission experience.

So the lingering question is: what are the marks of a mature convert? The example above shows how different cultural contexts measure the depth of one's conversion and maturity differently. Christians need to have a basic foundational understanding of conversion that helps them to embrace specific contextual issues of conversion. Contextualized discipleship integrates the scriptural foundation of conversion with contextual issues to make disciples competent in their own specific contexts in the light of the global body of Christ.

Fourth, not only cultural contexts but also theological traditions assign different meanings to conversion, and this complicates the issue. The dispute regarding "converting the converts" or "stealing of members" has been one of the results of a lack of consensus among Christians on the meaning of conversion. Kankanamalage writes,

> The lack of consensus on evangelism and conversion often leads
> to dismissive charges and counter-charges (sects, unbelievers,

proselytism) . . . Moreover, proselytism hinders the common witness and further widens Christian disunity. This situation requires the disciples of Jesus to seek mutual conversion before converting others.[18]

The ecumenical community has been in serious debate about who should be the target of conversion – insiders or outsiders or both? Not only at the institutional level but at an individual level too there is a difference in experience. Conversion stories are as numerous as the individuals who experienced them. The scope and the intensity of the conversions are different for different people. It is difficult to draw a universal experiential guide to conversion even from the Scripture. For instance, Paul had a miraculous dramatic conversion but the other apostles' experiences were not exactly the same as Paul's. For some it begins with emotional revival that adds joy and excitement to their souls, for others it is an intellectual turn-around that leads them to a deeper understanding of the truth, and still others see it as connecting to a community that provides them with a new identity that is meaningful to their existence. David Wells's explanation of conversion sheds light on the above discussion. According to Wells,

> "Insider conversion" refers to people who have a substantial set of beliefs before coming to Christ, for example, Jews who believe in the Old Testament, children of Christian homes, churchgoers who accept the basic biblical truths but who lack a personal relationship with Christ. "Outsider conversion" refers to people who have little or no prior knowledge of Christianity and who may need to repudiate a larger set of beliefs and practices before Christian conversion is possible. Such beliefs would include non-Christian religions such as Hinduism, Islam . . . alien ideologies . . . Marxism and Western secularism, whose relativity and materialism constitute another form of idolatry.[19]

As the backgrounds of people differ, their conversion experiences will also differ. Teaching on discipleship has to take this into consideration. Understanding the pre-conversion background of our converts helps us to design their discipleship training. The questions that insiders ask are not identical to the questions of outsiders. However, people are in different stages

---

18. Kankanamalage, "Conversion and Proselytism," 111.
19. Wells, *Turning to God*, 29.

in their understanding about God and there should always be desire to be changed and helped by God.

Christian conversion is different from other social or political conversions in that it has a divine element through the work of the Holy Spirit. The spiritual journey begins with finding the truth in Christ that connects with the community of disciples. Conversion, as Jesus described it, is a "born again" experience. It is a new beginning to a new life in a new spiritual realm. As a physical birth happens in a biological family, spiritual birth takes place in a spiritual family context. However, anthropologists downplay the role of divine involvement in conversion and attribute it mainly to socio-economic factors and motivations. It would be useful to mention some of the perspectives on the meaning and causes of conversion from different disciplines.

Different Perspectives on Conversion

Because of its complex nature, conversion is defined and understood differently in different disciplines. The biblical understanding is different from some of the psychological and anthropological explanations of conversion. First, I will briefly discuss conversion from a psychological perspective. Psychologists define conversion as a result of an internal crisis of an individual or a desperation that forces one to look for answers outside oneself. They focus on the mental dimension of individuals that is internal and personal. On one hand, they perceive conversion as "a result of abnormal experiences that have their origin in a malfunctioning brain,"[20] and on the other hand as a normal activity responding to a life crisis whether it is physical, fear, frustration or mental distress. Dong Young Kim writes,

> Conversion has been regarded as regressive psychopathology, a process of unifying the divided self, an experience of intellectual arousal and cognitive satisfaction, or a part of the positive human development process. On the whole, psychological studies of conversion have primarily emphasized the convert's inner crisis, need, and mental development/fulfillment.[21]

From a psychological perspective, it is a human attempt to deal with personal, relational and mental issues. Therefore, individuals seek conversion when they are faced with challenges and the existing setting fails to solve the problem.

---

20. Malony and Southard, *Handbook*, 149.
21. Kim, *Understanding*, 32.

Conversion is perceived as dealing with one's mental, emotional or identity crisis that might be caused by a developmental stage or external pressures.

Regarding sudden conversion, psychologists believe that it is not an intelligent response but an emotional one that does not last long. "Sudden converts tended to be more emotional, subject to mood swing, excitable, fearful, and showed relatively less independence and creativity."[22] It is true that emotion is involved in conversion, but the psychologists totally bypass the divine involvement in the conversion process. It is difficult to explain conversion as a merely human attempt to change one's situation. Some extraordinary experiences will not fall into the categories given in the psychological explanation. However, it is true that conversion happens a lot in the context of socio-political crisis. When people are hopeless, perhaps facing a fatal illness or other life crisis, they often turn to God for answers. God uses these moments to draw people near to himself. In the history of Christian conversion individual and community conversion has been reported in the presence of an economic crisis, or a disease epidemic. The growth of the African church can be partly attributed to the socio-economic crisis that is rampant in the continent. Yet explaining conversion from a human mental point of view fails to capture the entire process of human change.

Second, from a sociological perspective, conversion is a result of social mistreatment or rejection of certain individuals or groups. When the person is frustrated with his society or the existing socio-cultural structure, he or she decides to make a change. If the alternative group is more accepting and inclusive, the individual's conversion is imminent. Kim writes, "Conversion has been viewed as a resolution of enduring personal frustration or deprivation through religious affiliation, a result of interpretation bonds and social networks, or a product of the effectiveness of institutional recruitment strategies."[23]

The social network is crucial in the process of conversion and stabilization of one's decision. The community gives the convert a new setting and identity, which solidifies and strengthens the decision he or she has made. Sociologists place great emphasis on the necessity of the social environment for conversion and transformation. The community gives structure and framework, as conversion is a product of conversation and engagement in a community. For the sociologist it is the motivation and influence of the community that leads to conversion of an individual or group. In general, the consensus of sociologists

22. Ibid., 19.
23. Ibid., 45.

is that conversion lives and dies with its immediate and wider community. In their view, the approach or the recruitment system of the church or institution contributes a lot to the response of the individual.

The contribution of sociologists to the understanding of conversion is that conversion requires a strong social network that initiates continuous conversion of the individual. The point to take from this perspective is,

> . . . how significant other people in the religious communities/ institutions have provided love, support, and belonging to make up for the potential convert's frustration with his/her deprivation in the social and cultural condition of his or her time as well as to mold and confirm the values, expectations, and beliefs of religious groups.[24]

Kim highlights the role of the community in facilitating the conversion and solidifying the decision of the individual convert. The need for contextual community is crucial because the community shapes the new convert's values and worldviews. Sociologists believe that the strength of the convert's commitment depends on the community that embraces him or her.

Third, conversion from a biblical perspective focuses on turning from the sinful life to the grace of God. It is a decision to follow Christ and involves a change of allegiance. It is a decision that affects everything in the life of the convert. Paul the apostle saw his conversion as a major incident in his life; he included his conversion story in his preaching of the gospel at least twice (Acts 22 and 26). The biblical perspective on conversion adds the divine dimension to the human element in that God takes the initiative to offer his grace to sinners.

In the Old Testament, the idea of conversion is used for Israelites to return to God and repent of their sins (Hos 6:1; Exod 4:7). The Israelites continually rebelled against God, and that brought punishment from God that sent them to captivity, but God was always patient with them and waited with outstretched hands to receive them if they would repent and return to him. Gillespie writes,

> For the Hebrew, conversion was not just the experience of changing, but included a goal of action on the part of the believer where the conception of God's will was being fulfilled in turning around. It was movement back to knowing God. This movement had religious implications and was true religious conversion. Conversion involves not only repentance of one's sins but it also

---

24. Ibid.

requires a movement towards knowing God's will and living accordingly. It is a decision that requires a continuous journey towards living that decision daily.[25]

The New Testament concept of conversion is a continuation of the Old Testament understanding of relationship between God and his people. According to Gillespie the Old Testament concept of conversion goes beyond just turning around. It has a strong element of going forward in the direction of God's will and commitment to live accordingly. For this to happen humanity needs God's help. The fallen nature of human beings cannot change itself. It needs the power and grace of God to be extended so humanity can respond. Christian conversion is an individual or communal response to the call of the Holy Spirit (and to the witness of the believing community) to receive eternal life by repentance and faith. Conversion is a decision to accept God's grace and to allow oneself to be changed by it. Gillespie writes,

> It seems that the primary biblical viewpoint regarding a definition of religious conversion is that it means a change, a turning around from and to a viewpoint, or a return to the principles of God. Conversion is a thorough-going turn-around, with the reorientation to the reality of life.[26]

From the convert's viewpoint it is a voluntary submission in repentance because God has provided the way of salvation. Conversion is not about getting the steps or the rituals right; it is an acknowledgement of what God has done through Christ and a total submission in response. The convert has to focus on the eternal reward rather than any earthly blessings. It is a decision to respond to the divine initiative but it also requires a continuous living by the grace of God that affects one's personal and relational life. Conversion is about all we have and all of our future.

Conversion from the biblical perspective goes beyond personal crisis and sociological adjustment; it is a positive response to God's call to turn away from sin. Turning to God and walking with him is what a discipleship journey entails. The initial experience or moment of conversion is an entry to a subsequent way of life that is determined by what the individual has "turned to." Kasdorf rightly commented,

---

25. Gillespie, *Religious Conversion*, 13.

26. Ibid., 16.

Thus the basic meaning of the term *metanoia* is "to have a change
of mind, it being an altered attitude toward sin . . . repentance
involves a change of total person – mind, heart and will. It means
to take a new direction in life. It means to give up the old life and
enter upon a new life."[27]

Here the emphasis is on turning away or changing of mind. It is turning
to God with all our mind, strength and actions to follow him continually.
Conversion is personal and internal; it is social and communal, and it is divine
and spiritual. It involves the entire person and directs the entire life of the
individual. It goes deeper than just a change of attitude and relationship. Henri
Gooren writes, "The end result is supposed to be a change of mind and a
change of heart. Perhaps we could call it, in contemporary terms, a change of
identity."[28] Conversion affects one's identity, relationship and purpose in life.
In the conversion process, the core question is not the incident itself but the
outcome of the conversion. It is important to clearly identify what believers
are converted to. As Jonathan Dodson rightly comments, "It is also important
to consider *what man is converted to*. The gospel converts our hearts, minds,
and money, but it also converts us to something. We are converted to Christ,
to church, and to mission."[29] Causes for Christian conversion may be found
in internal and external life crises, but ultimately God initiates and empowers
the individual through his Spirit to respond positively to fellowship with him
in eternal relationship. It is an entry point and a demarcation line where the
believer begins his or her discipleship journey.

From these perspectives on conversion, we can deduce that conversion is
a divinely initiated human response. The role of community in actualization of
the conversion is also monumental. It is both an event and a process where the
individual continues to convert holistically. On the basis of this understanding,
I will discuss the approaches to conversion that may inform the discipleship
process of believers.

Different Approaches to Conversion

Our approach to conversion sets the stage for our discipleship journey as a
community. On the basis of our approach we design our program and plans of

27. Kasdorf, *Christian Conversion*, 16.
28. Gooren, *Religious Conversion*, 10.
29. Dodson, *Gospel*, 108.

discipleship. Churches and institutions approach discipleship in the following different ways. Let me mention the three common approaches:

First, one can approach conversion as a complex process deeper than just a one-time event. One can understand conversion as a dramatic encounter with the divine that changes everything in one's life. But the dramatic encounter is just the beginning, not an end in itself. Rambo writes,

> Conversion is a process of religious change that takes place in a dynamic force field of people, events, ideologies, institutions, expectations, and orientations . . . Conversion is a process over time, not a single event . . . Conversion is contextual and thereby influences and is influenced by a matrix of relationships, expectations and situations . . . factors in the conversion process are multiple, interactive, and cumulative.[30]

Conversion is a dynamic process that requires time, a conducive environment and factors that catalyze the process. The missiological significance of this approach is that converts to Christ, despite their conversion stories, need continual instruction and follow-up to continue the growth process. The convert's testimony of divine encounter has to be taken as a stepping-stone for the discipleship journey, not as an end in itself.

Paul Hiebert, in his essay on conversion, discusses two approaches to understanding conversion, namely bounded set and centered set. The bounded set approach as explained by Hiebert is that, "we determine who is Christian and who is not and to keep the two sharply differentiated."[31] From such a perspective, conversion is meeting a certain standard and being qualified to be an insider. According to the bounded set, there is a bold straight line that demarcates who is in and who is out. The centered set, on the other hand, places God at the center of the spiritual journey and every believer as on a journey towards the center. Unlike the bounded set it does not put people in boxes of outs and ins. For centered set conversion, "having turned around, one must continue to move towards the center."[32] In the centered set approach, the emphasis is not on the conversion moment but on the continual momentum of growth. The dramatic experiences might mean a beginning point or a springboard for one to continue to build on but it cannot be everything. Gillespie quotes Berger, emphasizing conversion as a process: "To have a

---

30. Rambo, *Understanding*, 5.

31. Hiebert, "Conversion in Cross-Cultural Perspective," 94.

32. Ibid., 97.

conversion experience is nothing much. The real thing is to be able to keep on taking it seriously; to retain a sense of its plausibility."[33] The convert's experience requires theological cultivation and shaping through continual instruction of the Word of God; otherwise, it will fade away and lose its meaning.

Conversion is a process in that human beings have different dimensions of life that need to be considered in the discipleship process. For instance, one might be convinced rationally or logically but without passion or love for the cause. Others, on the other hand, may respond emotionally without any logical reasoning. But both kinds of converts, through the process of continual learning, add other dimensions to their primary conviction. Intellectual converts may add passion and experience to their logic, and these provide a more stable ground for the process.

If we accept conversion as a process and the centered set as a model, group conversion should be considered as one of the ways believers enter into the discipleship journey, because the emphasis is not on the initial experience of the individual but on the commitment afterwards. From the Western perspective, conversion is a personal decision of the individual; otherwise it could be perceived as an imposition or a violation of one's rights. The individual makes a personal decision and he or she is responsible for it. However, in many non-Western cultures decisions are made in community, even if the whole community does not agree. In a communal culture, the deviant suffers isolation and rejection by the community.

In the non-Western cultures, an individual decision is not only punished severely but also brings social crisis. An individual's decision without the backing of the community always becomes a difficult hill to climb. The community might have little or no understanding about their new adventure; it may be decided by the leaders of the community without the consensus of its members, but the community's willingness to start the spiritual journey has to be understood as an opportunity to begin the discipleship process. In Kim's words, conversion is "an ongoing process – with . . . a series of important moments of perspective-altering conviction and illumination – through which people (or a group) gradually bring the lived story of their lives into congruence with the core story of Christian faith."[34]

Conversion is less than complete at the beginning stages. Through continuous follow-up and teaching the conversion takes root in the hearts

---

33. Gillespie, *Religious Conversion*, 3.

34. Kim, *Understanding*, 31.

and minds of individual converts or groups. Having said that, for those who have made their decision in groups there should be individual mentoring and discipleship training to further cement their decision. At the end of the day, our daily walk with Christ involves individual decisions. A balanced approach is important, in which the community does not override the individual's commitment and the individual does not isolate himself and his decision.

As Mark Spindler rightly comments, we should not override the individual's rights and responsibilities, but we should perceive people as individuals. He writes,

> As individuals-in-society, maybe; as individuals-in-context, of course; but at any rate as individuals, shaped and created individually, separated from their mothers at birth, and dying alone, each for himself or herself is called to a living dialogue with God in Christ.[35]

Individuals are accountable for their sins and actions. A communal decision has to be backed by individual commitment to the discipleship process. One of the challenges in African Christianity is due to the fact that many converts have come to Christ through a communal decision and with lack of discipleship; consequently there has been a failure to transform the individual lives. Communal decision-making also works against Christianity, for if the community decides to return to their traditional beliefs everyone has to agree. Though we accept people who come to faith in groups, their continuous journey of discipleship should be based on Scripture, not on what the community agrees to do.

Second, one can approach conversion as a multidimensional and holistic process. Our human lives have many dimensions that the light of the gospel needs to address gradually. We have to bring the entire social, spiritual, behavioral and intellectual dimensions of life under the lordship of Christ. For instance, one of the challenges of tribal communities is dealing with ethnocentrism. If conversion in such contexts fails to address the relationship issue from a scriptural perspective in challenging the existing attitude towards other tribes, conflicts are unavoidable. Kasdrof writes that "conversion in a specific regard to community means turning from ethnicity, tribalism, to . . . Jesus' lordship (within the church) and from geographical and temporal parochialism (nationalism) to the universal (present and coming) kingdom."[36]

---

35. Spindler, "Conversion Revisited," 299.
36. Kasdorf, *Christian Conversion*, 23.

People in tribal communities need to be confronted with the scriptural concept that all people are created in the image of God and deserve equal treatment. Cultures have different layers that all need thorough transformation, and therefore holistic conversion requires a multidimensional approach. Let me raise an issue regarding theological training in Africa: much theological training is based on an intellectual and academic view of education. In such situations lectures, seminars and debates on academic issues and theories are the primary media of communication, and the practical and behavioral aspects of training do not get due attention. The evaluation is limited to assessing certain skills and knowledge rather than development of the whole person. Therefore, if the graduates fail in their ministry, it is not only because of their personal weakness but also because of the ineffectiveness of the training methodology. The information that a person receives in theological education does not guarantee transformation because there are other factors that contribute to the process of conversion.

In their discussion about post-conversion personality change, Paloutzian, Richardson, and Rambo et al. describe three levels of conversion. Level one concerns basic personal traits and temperaments such as introversion and extroversion, which, according to the research, continues unchanged in the course of conversion. Level two is concerned with "aspects of personal functioning – particular ways that a person expresses his or her traits or adapts to diverse situations in the real world."[37] These aspects of the person change with religious conversion. The third level goes deeper, and is concerned with personal identity and self-definition, which are subject to change in the process of conversion. These levels need a step-by-step continuous encounter and engagement in order to result in comprehensive conversion.

David Couturier in his book *The Four Conversions* argues that for transformation to happen in the lives of individuals and communities there has to be a holistic conversion that comprises personal, interpersonal, ecclesial and structural elements. He writes that transformation requires

> . . . a holistic and integrated plan of conversion in four mutually enriching and interdependent phases. The four zones of conversion – personal, interpersonal, ecclesial and structural – provide us with a richer understanding of the challenge we face as individuals and as communities as we try to respond to the

---

37. Paloutizian, Richardson, and Rambo et al., "Religious Conversion," 1068.

gospel call to love God with our hearts, minds, and souls and our neighbor as ourselves.[38]

These four dimensions begin with personal conversion that comes because of encounter with the divine or with human agents. Conversion at the interpersonal stage deals with the dynamics of relationship with others and creation in general. At the ecclesial stage, it is about a conversion towards the community of Christ, and finally the structural conversion is about a change in specific organizational life. In short, conversion has many stages, dimensions and angles, which makes it complex and requires a multidimensional approach.

Third, conversion can be seen as a life change rather than a culture change. Mission during the colonial era targeted culture, mainly to civilize the cultures of the non-Western world. This program aimed to replace the superstitious culture of the "pagan" world with the civilized Christian culture. Conversion was concerned more about changing culture than with changing lives. The response of the indigenous people to such pressure was an accommodation of both cultures and religions in trying to live in two worlds. Culture, being a way of living designed by the community and transferred from generation to generation, has a strong grip on people. An attempt to root out culture from a society is almost an impossible task. Culture has to be transformed not replaced. To transform culture one has to transform the individuals who own the culture. Gillespie rightly observed, "It seems that religious conversion would not be as likely to occur if the culture or society's traditions did not expect it to occur."[39] If the people are confronted with the gospel, they expect and lead the change in culture. But replacing one culture with another will not solve the problem of sin. Sin is in every human culture and the gospel has to deal with the social evils in all cultures. Christ was incarnated in human culture and his target was not to abolish culture but to transform it.

As mentioned above, biblical conversion is about life in its totality, not just about culture. It is a change in direction of life from sinfulness to righteousness by the grace of God. A person who has a cultural conversion might continue to practice other cultures while retaining a sinful life. Western culture, though it may be civilized, is not sinless, and African culture, however uncivilized it appears, is not all devilish. In the past converts were expected to make a cultural change on top of the religious change. In some cases, that practice isolated believers from their communities and closed the door on witnessing

---

38. Couturier, *Four Conversions*, 5.
39. Gillespie, *Dynamics of Religious Conversion*, 98.

opportunities. In the discipleship journey the believing community will be equipped to change, replace and transform their culture to reflect the kingdom of God.

This process requires contextualization done by the community, not by imposition of missionaries or outsiders. For instance, among the Hamar of southern Ethiopia, one of the obstacles in their conversion to Christianity concerned their style of dress. The highlander evangelists, who understood Western dress as one of the signs of conversion in their own culture, forced the pastoralist groups to change their dress style. These and other external requirements became a hindrance to the advancement of the gospel. As a result, conversion to Christianity was perceived as converting to a different ethnic group or culture. But the Scripture teaches that conversion is not a change of garment but a change of heart (2 Cor 5:17). A person with traditional clothing but a new heart is a new creation in the Spirit.

Psychologists and anthropologists interpret conversion as a human initiative and effort but theologians emphasize God's grace as the key element in the conversion of individuals. It is by grace that a sinful human being gets strength to respond positively to the offer of God. The grace of God mends even those wrongly motivated conversions. Buckser and Glazier write,

> Conversion is . . . possibly experimental at first, it becomes a deliberate change with definite direction shape. It shows itself responsive to a particular knowledge and practices. To be converted is to re-identify, to learn, reorder, and reorient. It involves interrelated modes of transformation that generally continues over time and defines a consistent course.[40]

In summary, Christian conversion is a complex multidimensional process that begins with the initiation of the Spirit and a response from humanity in turning away from sin towards God and growing continuously towards the likeness of Christ through a discipleship process.

Contextualization of Conversion

Christian conversion has to be biblically defined and contextually expressed as the community lives and witnesses to Christ, influencing their society as they advance the kingdom of God. What is the implication of all the discussion above

---

40. Buckser and Glazier, *Anthropology*, 2.

for the global churches? In other words, beyond the meaning of conversion and different approaches or perspectives, how should the church act?

> The deeper question . . . is, what does "born again" mean in our culture? Where is the evidence of conversion in the personal and corporate lifestyles of God's people? How does the "born again" experience reflect itself in the values of the society . . . is it a private faith unrelated to morality?[41]

Conversion that does not influence the lives of individuals and the community has fallen short of its purpose. The integration of the divine encounter with the journey of the believing community towards maturity should work towards the betterment of the society and transformation of its culture. Conversion that is biblically sound leads to practical action not as a requirement but as an expression of inner transformation.

Lewis Rambo in his book *Understanding Religious Conversion* explores stages of conversion. He approaches conversion as a process; he maps out different stages in religious conversion. These stages are: context, crisis, quest, encounter, interaction, commitment, and consequences. Rambo's classification, though it has seven stages, can be grouped into three key levels. Context, crisis and quest can be grouped under the category of context. The three concepts have similarities in that they all concern personal, social, and geographical circumstances. They are descriptive concepts of a situation or status of an individual, or a community. These concepts are interrelated as one leads to another. Context creates crisis in the lives of people and crisis ignites questions that in turn force people to search for answers. From a missiological perspective, context, crisis and questions are the main subjects of contextualization because contextualization begins by understanding the issues, concerns and the reality on the ground. It exegetes the socio-political and relational context of the community. For missionaries this is where learning the culture, language, social structure and customs is of benefit in connecting with the context.

In understanding the context, the missionary can tailor his or her message accordingly. People are attracted to solutions that are provided to address their contextual issues rather than those dealing with unrelated topics. Studies done on the motivation of conversion show that people always think in terms of the benefits gained from their decisions. According to Longo and Kim-Spoon, what drives apostates and converts is deprivation (economic, social, organismic, ethical and psychic), an expectation of reward because of their conversion,

---

41. Schmidt, *Conversion*, 3.

and social attachment that gives an identity to the convert.[42] The above driving factors of conversion can be different in different social contexts. Therefore, understanding the context gives us relevant data for our conversation with the individuals in the culture and for rereading of the Scripture.

Rambo's stages four and five are encounter and interaction respectively, which I would like to call contextualization. According to Rambo, this is a stage in which people in crisis search for solutions, and encounter human and supernatural agents of change. The encounter stage is followed by the interaction stage, where the continuation of dynamic discourse takes place between the searcher and the solutions offered. Contextualization is encountering people and interacting with them in sharing solutions from the Scriptures. Tim Keller writes,

> Contextualization is giving people *the Bible's answers*, which they may not at all want to hear, *to questions about life* that people in their particular time and place are asking, *in language and forms* they can comprehend, and *through appeals and arguments* with force they can feel, even if they reject them. (Italics in original)[43]

Effective encounter and interaction can only happen when we share the right message, speak in the language of the context and address the needs of the people. This is contextualization: a dialogue between the text and context.

Rambo's last two stages are commitment and consequences, where the convert's decision is strengthened and solidified and bears the fruit of transformation. I call this stage a discipleship process, where the individual believer grows and matures as he or she becomes a disciple and a disciple maker. Regarding the importance of the liminal time in the life of the convert M. Eliade writes,

> The liminal phase is a *chaotic* time precisely because it abolishes all socially sanctioned identities, statuses, and roles. With reality suspended, clear guidelines for action and clues of identity vanish. Initiates die to the old order and are not yet resurrected to the new. Their guides and instructors, seasoned and skilled in the ways of their people, enhance the chaotic quality of this liminal

---

42. Longo and Kim-Spoon, "What Drives Apostates."
43. Keller, *Center Church*, 98.

state by submitting initiates to ordeals surrounded by symbols of womb and tomb.[44]

The liminal stage takes a person out of their familiar structure, out of their comfort zone, and makes them as vulnerable as a child. This is a crucial time for the church to step in and connect them with Christ. Otherwise, people either backslide or remain spiritually retarded in the church. Churches often lose their new converts because of their ineffective strategies of discipleship. There is often a great joy when someone is added to the church as a convert, but without proper discipleship, mission is incomplete. The leaders, pastors and ministers of the church should work together to meet people at their crisis stage and build them up in biblical teaching to grow towards spiritual maturity (see fig. 2).

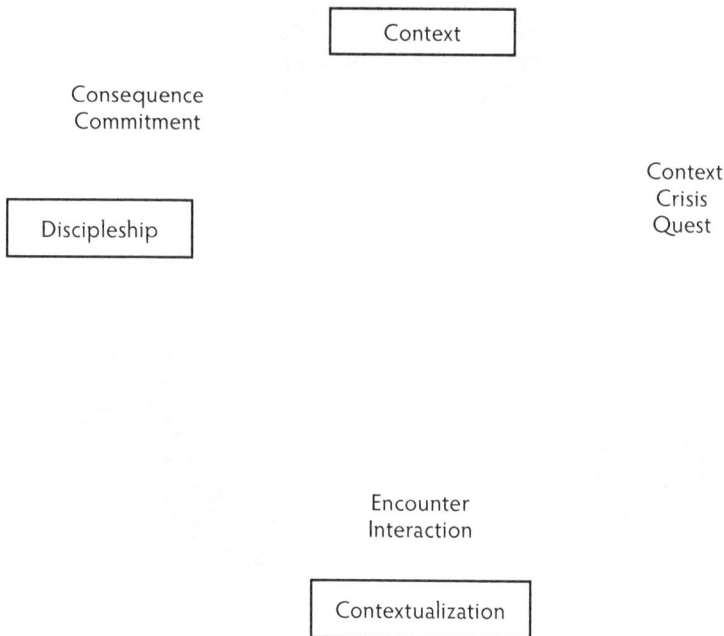

Context

Consequence
Commitment

Context
Crisis
Quest

Discipleship

Encounter
Interaction

Contextualization

Figure 2. Stages of Conversion (Adapted from Lewis Rambo)

Humanity faces crises constantly on account of its fallen nature. The lives of individuals are filled with unanswered and unsolved ultimate questions which

---

44. Eliade, *Patterns*, 35–37.

are difficult for anyone to answer. Technology has tried, but it is more than human civilization can handle. Philosophers have proposed different solutions, but all in vain. However, God through Christ Jesus has given an ultimate answer for the ultimate questions of human life and death. God encountered the world by sending his son to die for the world. God continues to interact with humanity through his Word and Spirit. The church is an agent of God in presenting the gospel to the world in ways that they can hear and respond to. When people come to Christ with genuine conversion, his grace sets them free from the bondage of sin and gives them the privilege of being in the family of God. A disciple enters the spiritual journey through a crucial life decision and continues to grow in a balanced life that reflects Christ in every dimension. As Spindler puts it,

> "Fellowship" minus the passion for conversion leads to ghettoism, "service" minus the call to conversion is a gesture without hope, "Christian education" minus conversion is religiosity without decision, and "dialogue" without challenge to conversion remains sterile talk.[45]

---

45. Spindler, "Conversion Revisited," 302.

4

Rituals Intensify the Discipleship Journey

R ituals are the mother tongue of religion![1] Every people group has a culture, every culture has a religion, every religion has a ritual, and rituals have symbols. According to anthropologists, religion is key to culture and ritual is key to religion.[2] Human beings live and function in rituals. Different institutions, societies, religions, and political organizations have different rituals that people are required to perform. Numerous studies have been done on understanding and explaining rituals. Earlier psychologists such as Freud related rituals to emotional feelings of guilt, whereas Durkheim and Geertz thought of rituals as practical components of religion. Leach and Strauss define ritual as a medium of communication and Strecker and Turner relate ritual to power control and rebellion against structure.[3]

In addition, Arnold Van Gennep's classic work entitled *The Rites of Passage* contributed to the understanding of rituals and their role in transforming individuals and the community. However, although rituals are an important part of religious experience the theological understanding of rituals has not progressed to the same extent as anthropological studies of rituals. To mention a few monumental works: Zahniser's *Symbol and Ceremonies* is an informative and contextualized approach to rituals in regard to making disciples across cultures. Gerard Lukken discusses the contemporary situation of rituals and their role in a society.[4]

---

1. Jetter, *Symbol and Ritual*, 93, quoted by Lukken, *Rituals*, 150.
2. Segal, "Victor Turner's Theory," 327.
3. Mamo, "Knowing God."
4. Lukken, *Rituals*.

Handling rituals requires wisdom and understanding, for misunderstanding the role of rituals can easily lead a community to syncretism and legalism. When people stick to ritual more than to God, they become an idolatrous community, as happened in the Old Testament building of Aaron's calf (Exod 32:1–6). God has never intended a ritual that obscures his relationship with his people; rather, rituals that God has ordained illustrate or solidify the recognition of his lordship over his people. Aaron's calf disrupted God's relationship with his people and brought judgment on the people. Rituals applied wrongly can lead God's people in wrong directions.

Christians perform many rituals in the church. The main sacraments common in most denominations are baptism, communion, and wedding and burial ceremonies, but there are other rituals that are included in Christian meetings. After conversion, a Christian life is energized by rituals that strengthen and intensify the spiritual journey. These rituals have to be contextualized and integrated in the spiritual journey of the believer to give deeper understanding. Let me begin with the following observation with regards to contextualizing rituals. Rituals are the least incorporated and the most misunderstood elements in the discipleship process of believers, so they need urgent attention. First, missionaries and evangelists were afraid to incorporate indigenous rituals because of their complicated nature. Rather than dealing with traditional rituals and exploring their meanings, believers preferred to replace them with other rituals from different contexts.

As an illustration I mention what happened among the Hamar regarding a worship service. Traditionally, the Hamar people meet and discuss issues in groups. It is never a monologue, but a democratic dialogue, where people express their thoughts according to their age from older to younger respectively. When Christianity was introduced the meetings turned into a monologue and younger people who were inexperienced in life took the leadership. During the sermons, there were times when the Hamar people were tempted to insert comments, but they were rebuked for interrupting the preaching. The traditional way of communal discourse was changed into a boring monologue. The effective cultural way of communication was discarded and replaced by strange rituals.

Heather Sharkey in her book entitled *The Unexpected Consequences of Christian Missionary Encounters* writes,

> In early colonial years, the missions made some inroads into the cultivation of a community of the local Christians. The Protestants focused on opening schools. They trained and paid groups of

African teachers who were their most loyal followers. The Catholics, by contrast, focused on eradicating "pagan" rituals and spreading the sacraments of baptism, confession and marriage.[5]

According to Sharkey, both Catholics and Protestants failed to understand the structure and the rituals of the indigenous people and introduced their way of communication and governance. As a result, people were participating in both church rituals and witchcraft purification rituals. When traditional rituals are replaced by meaningless rituals it breeds syncretism, where people practice additional rituals behind closed doors. When crisis hits, people turn to their old traditional rituals in secret. I remember a few believers in southern Ethiopia, where I grew up, who sent their relatives to visit the witchdoctors to inquire for them. Zahniser rightly understood the problem when he writes.

> Protestant disciplers thus left a vacuum that believers filled with magical practices and folk cures inherited from their traditional religion. It seems clear, then, that effective cross-cultural discipling requires working with symbols. And since, according to historian of religion Larry Shinn, rituals are symbols acted out, symbols must be basic to our cross-cultural discipling.[6]

One can mention many examples of the failure of Christian churches to appropriately contextualize rituals. The point is that rituals need an appropriate contextualization to support the discipleship journey of the believers. With all the education and modernization of our global culture we cannot afford to ignore rituals.

Second, the complexity of rituals leads to diverse understanding of their role. Historically, churches have divided and fought over the meaning and the performance of rituals. This is one of the reasons why there are so many traditions in the church. Sometimes rituals are overemphasized, at other times underemphasized or ignored. The role and the function of baptism and communion is a disputed subject among many theologians. When to baptize – at childhood or as an adult – has been argued over for years. In addition to that, when the meaning of rituals is misunderstood or mixed with traditional religions, it creates confusion in the minds of believers. For example, southern Ethiopia is the home of numerous rituals, and some exotic and fascinating

---

5. Sharkey, *Cultural Conversions*, 34.
6. Zahniser, "Ritual Process," 75.

rituals are practiced in the south. Sometimes the traditional understanding of religious rituals is extended to Christian rituals.

To illustrate my point: there is a myth, though not official, that if someone fails to be baptized after approaching the baptismal river (it happens either by the elders' decision or if the person is unable to answer the final oral interview question) it is a bad sign. Failure to perform rituals successfully is believed to bring wrath from the gods in the traditional religion. Because of this background myth, believers can be overly nervous when they approach the baptism river.

I remember that during my own baptism as a lad an elderly woman behind me was so nervous that she could not give the right answer to the interview question. She was almost disqualified; however, they interviewed her several times and finally she made it. As I recall, the questions were: What comes first, faith or baptism? What saves, faith or baptism? One has to respond that faith in Christ saves and comes first. Many of the converts in the south know the rituals and the role of rituals in traditional religion. They also know how punishable it is to fail in the process of doing rituals. The Christian rituals are not about punishment; they are about joyful experience of God's love and grace. Christian rituals are manifestations of God's grace, not his wrath. Irma Dueck writes,

> Rituals such as baptism are participatory experiences that enable believers to move from concrete reality, in which water is just water, to another reality, in which water carries the believer into a world hidden beyond the world of facts and rationality and beyond a linear understanding of time. In baptism, believers are submerged in the reality of God and in the new creation; they are immersed in the grace, love, and mystery of God.[7]

It should be a joyous moment for believers as they receive the grace, love and mystery of God. The contextualization of Christian ritual is important not only to correct misunderstandings but to deepen the understanding of the gospel.

Third, rituals are facing challenges in the changing global culture. With the change of culture, the role of rituals is also changing. On one hand, the younger generation is tired of static rituals and structures; on the other hand, new rituals are continually introduced through the media and pop culture. Due to individualism and secularism Christian rituals are losing their communal meaning. To worsen things, charismatic preachers have introduced all sorts

---

7. Dueck, "It's Only Water," 24.

of new rituals that shelve the main sacraments of the mainline churches. For instance, anointed materials, oil and other objects are on sale in many charismatic churches. Popular preachers' pictures or televised healing services are more desired than communion services in the mainline churches. Rituals are supposed to integrate the convert to the community, but that is not taking place in many congregations. Unfortunately, rituals are misunderstood, neglected, or overused. The body of Christ is not appropriately using the rituals for the glory of God and the benefit of the believers.

Defining ritual is a daunting task. Rituals are everywhere, and we know them, but they are difficult to define. From the day of our birth to the day of our death, we encounter many rituals whether we are secular or religious. First, rituals are a media of communication. They are symbols and actions that people use to communicate and express their thoughts and feelings in a culturally appropriate way. They appear to be simple and familiar but they are complex and multi-vocal. According to Zahniser,

> . . . ritual condenses meanings, unifies diverse things and actions, and holds together dynamic tension (polarity) for personal transformation as well as community bonding. Rituals are administered by ritual experts who are eligible to conduct and lead the process. Rituals employ symbols and signs that serve as communication tools for rituals.[8]

As mentioned by Zahniser, rituals serve our communication attempts from many angles. In attaching multiple meanings to an event and integrating thoughts with experience, rituals uplift communication to a different level. Besides that, they are powerful in bonding the community as members enter into communal experience. We should realize that as the role of rituals diminishes in our communication so does our effectiveness in getting our message over. Chidester defines ritual as follows:

> Ritual is (1) symbolic action (2) that transmits a certain power (3) through natural symbols (4) which transforms the participants' experience of time and space (5) in the face of human limit situations. A ritual through its symbolic and natural objects helps the participants to experience the supernatural and mystical.[9]

---

8. Zahniser, *Symbol*, 78.
9. Chidester, "Challenge to Christian Ritual," 23.

Beyond the communication factor, Chidester emphasizes the power of rituals to transform the lives of individuals. If it is true that rituals transport the community beyond time and space into the spiritual and mystical, one can imagine how important Christian rituals can be to disciples of Christ in their journey to face challenges and overcome them.

Second, rituals serve as a mechanism to experience, define, and control the political and the spiritual world. They guide people's interaction with the world around. Rituals offer views through which we see our world and interpret it. H. Anderson defines ritual as follows:

> Ritual is an interpretative act through which we express and create meaning in our lives. We employ rituals for establishing courtship, diminishing powerlessness, organizing the hunt, caring for offspring, sending children off, avoiding life-threatening conflicts, and closing the story of a life. Rituals often evolve in surprising ways and illumine aspects of our lives never before understood.[10]

In every stage of our lives rituals accompany us to smooth out our transitions. Rituals shed light on the meaning of life and its course. We seek meaning and understanding in our interaction with our environment, and rituals bridge the gap between the reality of life and its meaning.

Third, ritual is an outward expression of inward conviction. In ritual the mystical is downsized into the concrete; the far is brought near to be touched and felt. That does not mean that rituals are just about physical experience. They are external demonstrations of internal conviction. That is why making sense of rituals requires a deeper understanding of the rituals and the cultural myths behind them. External observers can mistakenly condemn or praise a ritual if their assessment is based only on the actions or external aspects of the ritual. For example, the Hamar ritual of initiation appears to be brutal and painful. It attracted the attention of many anthropologists and tourists from all over the world, and the ritual is categorized as a harmful ritual by the Ethiopian government. During the initiation of a young boy, all the friends of the initiate flog the women of his clan severely.[11] For outsiders who observe the bloody scene it is a horrible abuse of women. It sickens the observers who watch the pain the women put up with to make the initiate happy. A few years ago, the

---

10. Anderson, "How Rituals Heal," 41.

11. *Atsa* is an initiation ritual that involves lots of flogging and beating of women. It is categorized as one of the harmful rituals by the government, but the community refused to give up the ritual.

local government decided to stop the practice and called a meeting with the community. The agenda was to stop the ritual. The women of the tribe replied,

> This is how we show our solidarity with the initiate. This ritual proves how brave and strong we are as women. We do not go to war as our men, but this is how we prove our toughness. The pain not only bonds us together as a clan but also gives us our place and identity in the society. Therefore, you better kill us all [rather] than banning this ritual.[12]

The government officials were shocked to hear that response from the assumed victims of the ritual and decided to educate the community and help them come to a decision. What might appear a horrible abuse of women is actually a promotion of women and an opportunity to prove that they are warriors too as their husbands are. Not only is there a status change of the family member in the ritual, but there is also an anti-structure protest or power struggle manifested in the ritual.

Community creates rituals, and in turn, rituals create a community. As people perform rituals or participate in rituals the process brings people together and creates bonds. There are a few private rituals, but ultimately the community has to witness and be involved in the ritual process in order for it to be effective. From social structure to relationship issues, from beliefs and values to identity transformation, rituals facilitate human communication.

In the religious context, rituals serve the following three purposes. First, rituals have a healing effect on participants. Humanity faces various pains, sorrows and sufferings. Loss of loved ones, or personal conflict, brings emotional and psychological pain to an individual or a community. Those emotions and frustrations can be channeled through rituals, which give people relief and closure. Rituals heal individuals and communities by containing emotions, consoling the hurting, connecting with others, creating a safe environment, and by fostering coherence in the specific context.[13] In the process of ritual people experience an emotional contentment and healing to continue with their lives as they process the loss. Second, rituals bring heaven to earth, the spiritual to the physical, and the divine to humanity. Humanity with its limited imagination naturally fails to experience the mystery of the other world, but rituals reconnect people to the mystical world. Lukken comments,

---

12. The response of a Hamar woman regarding the decision of the government to ban the initiation ritual reported by participant in the meeting, Turmi, Ethiopia, January 2010.

13. Anderson, "How Rituals Heal," 46.

> When rituals are not performed, experience of reality is lost, and this loss is all the more radical because it involves the impoverishment of an experience of reality that touches human experience as such. Rituals, after all, involve precisely the mystery of human reality: our person, our relations with others and with the world.[14]

Rituals bridge the gap between the spiritual and the physical. Rituals facilitate experiencing the reality, and loss of ritual makes things dry and un-engaging.

Third, the most important aspect of rituals for Christians is that they facilitate the discipleship of believers. Discipleship is a spiritual journey and so there is progression from stage to stage. These different stages can be marked by meaningful rituals that help the individual to grow deeper in his or her faith. Zahniser writes:

> [Discipleship] stresses ongoing initiation into the kingdom of God by instruction, experience, symbols, and ceremonies . . . Disciplers provide believers with lessons, experiences, symbols and ceremonies, facilitating their deeper and deeper entrance into the truth and life of the kingdom.[15]

Rituals serve as proper bridges between beliefs and behaviors. Through ritual experience the knowledge learned becomes the knowledge felt. Moreover, how rituals are performed in the culture can teach us how we can disciple others and create a community. If a ritual makes a positive contribution to the discipleship process, we can perhaps adopt it for Christianity. "In the agape, Christians adopted a ceremony from Judaism as a means of expressing and enhancing a central concept for their faith. If other religions can teach us discipling processes, they can also teach us discipling tools."[16] That does not mean we should copy indigenous rituals, but we can critically contextualize and use them to advance the kingdom of God and to make discipleship relevant in the context. Rituals are key to human relationships and communication in every cultural context. To correctly interpret signs and symbols used by the community we need to observe and learn how rituals work.

Christianity is not different from other religions in its use of rituals. Just as traditional religions have myths behind the rituals, Christian rituals carry

14. Lukken, *Rituals*, 133.

15. Zahniser, *Symbol*, 62.

16. Ibid., 63.

theological meaning. The Bible is a book of rituals and stories. For instance, in the book of Leviticus the Israelites performed numerous rituals of sacrifice; this shows how God communicated through rituals. In the New Testament Jesus used Jewish traditions and rituals to communicate the message of the gospel. For instance, the wedding incident in Cana (John 2) was a teaching moment in the context of an important ritual in Jewish life. Paul also used the fellowship meals in the Corinthian context to have a meaningful spiritual experience of communion table.

According to Zahniser, "the rite of passage from childhood to adulthood affects the bonding of meaning. As such it represents structure particularly useful for the discipling of a new or immature believer, particularly, though not exclusively, those from traditional religious backgrounds."[17] In the process of discipling believers, rituals can be integrated in at least two ways. First, the liminal period, where the convert is in the transitional stage, is an opportune time to instruct and mold the convert. As the convert deals with the life crisis of conversion, the discipler can walk closely with the convert to shape his or her life. As a child absorbs everything from adults, new converts at this time tend to absorb everything from whoever is mentoring them. It requires careful and integrated training to bring transformation. It is not good to rush converts into ministry before they understand the core message of the gospel. The liminal period has to be intentionally designed for learning, where it is culminated by ritual. Second, rituals should be critically contextualized to keep their biblical meaning intact and their cultural relevance alive. Rituals have to be integrated into the entire lives of believers, both inside and outside the four corners of the church building. The discipleship process has to be marked with rituals as milestones where the individual continues to grow in life and ministry. As the culture changes, the meaning and the role of rituals have to be continually appropriated and updated to speak to the contemporary culture.

Contextualizing Rituals for Discipleship

As human beings we are attached to our rituals. Intentionally or unintentionally we follow the rituals of our culture. "Smith argues that 'to be human is to use symbols'; namely, human persons use symbols to capture their identity, their important relationships, and even their deepest spiritual commitments."[18] One

17. Ibid., 4.
18. Kim, *Understanding*, 76.

of the controversial areas in mission is the integration of traditional indigenous rituals to Christianity. Participating in the indigenous ceremonies of unbelievers has divided Christians, some labelling others as liberals or extremists. On one hand anthropologists have painted a perfect picture of rituals and have fought to maintain them, and on the other hand, missionaries have demonized rituals and worked hard to change, replace or transform them.

During my research among the Hamar I met an anthropologist who refused to talk to me, accusing Christians and missionaries of changing the culture of the indigenous people. Rituals are battlegrounds because of their significance in the lives of the people. A missionary once asked an anthropologist to explain to him how the rituals function in the culture and the anthropologist replied, "You have asked me for a key to the heart of the community which I don't want you to have." Rituals can give us a road map to understand the socio-religious context, by which we can get access to speak to the hearts of the people. As we are called to bring everything under the lordship of Christ, rituals can be contextualized to serve the gospel as the people grow to maturity in Christ.

In the past missionaries and evangelists have tried to separate people from the rituals rather than to equip them to critically integrate the positive ones. As a result, Christian rituals were practiced with indigenous meaning, and what Zahniser calls split-level Christianity took place. He explains,

> On the level of the ultimate God and ultimate salvation issues, the members were practicing Christians. On the level of the issues that affected them in an intimate way day in and day out, such as protecting their village from disease, they continued to practice their traditional religion.[19]

One of the greatest obstacles for discipleship is a double life that appears to be good externally but is dead internally. In fact, people who have misunderstood the message of the gospel have set a bad example for discipleship that impedes the witness of the church. Zahniser writes, "Christian ritual does not derive its peculiar identity from excluding other meaningful rituals . . . but a Christian ritual has its place and shape in the midst of all other rituals . . . It is true that it does not merge into these other rituals, or there is a radical ritual pluralism."[20] Zahniser is right in that we don't have to monopolize rituals and trash all the other rituals; at the same time, we do not have to merge Christian rituals with

---

19. Zahniser, *Symbol*, 45.
20. Ibid., 525.

other rituals. Critical contextualization has to be applied to avoid syncretism that neither benefits believers nor glorifies God.

Baptism Contextualized

It would be helpful to take the ritual of baptism as an example to demonstrate how ritual has been contextualized in history and how it can be contextualized today. In evangelical tradition, it would be fair to describe baptism as a ritual that initiates believers into full membership of the church. In many denominations, after baptism, one has a voting right in church elections and may also be involved in ministry. The unbaptized members of the church are often seen as either immature believers or uncommitted Christians. Some traditions (the Lutherans, for example) baptize infants, but Baptists and Pentecostal churches do not recognize infant baptism. There are theological and historical arguments for and against the practice, but it is not my purpose to go into these here.

Baptism is not a new ritual introduced by Christianity. It was a practice of many religious institutions including Judaism. The word "baptism" was in Greek culture prior to the writings of the New Testament. "Long before the New Testament period the Greek word 'baptize' and its variants already had several meanings, but all of them derive from the single, most basic notion of the word, which was 'to dip, sink, or plunge into liquid.'"[21] John the Baptist and the early church continued the baptism ritual but with deeper theological meaning.

> Baptism had been practiced in Judaism for a long time before the time of Jesus as a ritual that cleansed one from impurity. Jesus himself was baptized by John "the Baptist" in the River Jordan. Therefore, the early followers of Jesus were just following a fairly common Jewish practice when they initiated new members into their community with a baptism.[22]

Baptism was practiced not only by Jews, but also by gentiles of that day. "The pagan cults of Bacchus, Isis, Mithras, and Serapis all included ritual immersions or washings described with the word 'baptize.'"[23]

Part of the early church's strategy for survival in suffering was taking the Christian ritual seriously in the discipleship process. The apostolic church went through severe persecution that could have wiped Christianity from the

---

21. Burton, "Baptism," 229.
22. Cooke and Macy, *Christian Symbol*, 70.
23. Ibid., 231.

face of the globe. It was a difficult time for Christians as they faced martyrdom and the risk of being thrown to the beasts in the Roman amphitheaters for their faith. Yet Christianity spread throughout the Mediterranean region and its influence reached as far as the Roman palace.

Thomas Finn argues that the reason Christianity thrived in such a hostile environment was their establishment of a dynamic ritual process. He writes,

> Christianity survived in Rome to large extent because they developed a dynamic ritual process for the making of Christians, technically called *catechumenate* . . . The catechumenate covered three years, involved two careful screenings, required daily oral instruction and prayer, emphasized exorcistic baptism and Eucharist.[24]

This process was holistic in that it included intellectual training, spiritual cleansing and emotional connection. As mentioned in Acts, the early believers were engaged in apostolic teaching (Acts 2:42). Renewing the mind of the converts with the transforming Word of God was their priority. They taught the converts daily with prayer in their social context. In relation to the converts' spiritual status, they conducted exorcism to see if any bondage was involved. To start the discipleship journey one has to be free from any demonic bondage. At the beginning, they examined the convert for his/her motives for joining Christianity. Afterwards, oral instruction continued with Bible lessons, liturgy and prayer at the end of every session. The ritual of baptism culminated the training process in which the convert was anointed with oil as a sign of the Spirit of God. Going through these rituals not only prepared the convert to integrate with the Christian community but also energized him/her to face persecution boldly.

Though Finn calls the *catechumenate* of the early church a ritual process, it is also a discipleship process that facilitated the growth of the early Christians as they contextually appropriated the commandment of Jesus to disciple the nations. In a persecuted church context, producing strong believers committed to die for their faith was not optional. In the three years of intensive training and discipling the convert was not only equipped in biblical concepts but was also shown how to live a consistent Christian life as practically demonstrated by the community of believers. No convert was allowed to enjoy the fellowship of believers without having the right knowledge and commitment. Baptism

---

24. Finn, "Ritual Process," 69–70.

served as the ritual of an ultimate covenant between the convert and God, and established unity with fellow believers.

> Baptism and confirmation are the matriculation and the incorporation of the baptized into the body of Christ, the church. Through baptism and confirmation, the Christian not only enters into association with the glorious humanity of the resurrected Christ – thus becoming a "real presence" of Christ, the Anointed of God – but he also enters into relation with all the baptized, all the members of the body of Christ.[25]

As Aghiorgoussis points out above, the uniqueness of the Christian baptism ritual is that the individual not only joins the local believing community but the body of Christ worldwide. Baptism places believers in their God-given position in the body of Christ from which they draw their identity and serve according to their gifts. The apostle Paul writes,

> We were buried therefore with him by baptism into death, in order that, just as Christ was raised from the dead by the glory of the Father, we too might walk in newness of life. For if we have been united with him in a death like his, we shall certainly be united with him in a resurrection like his. (Rom 6:4)

For Paul, baptism symbolizes dying with Christ as one goes under the water and rising with him as one comes out of the water. This concept calls the convert to more Christ-like living and greater commitment to his cause. Baptism reminds converts that because Christ died for them, they belong to him forever. Believers are called to die with Christ so that they can live with him. Paul incorporated the baptism ritual with the daily lives of believers and its significance to their spiritual lives.

However, though the meaning has not altered, the modes and procedures have been different in different historical and cultural contexts. The practice of baptism has been contextualized without changing its core meaning. In the following description of baptismal practice, we can observe the difference in the procedure and practical steps of baptism as it is shaped to address different issues in the context. Lukken writes,

> An important part of the baptismal ritual in the early church was the renouncing of Satan and sealing a covenant with Christ. Just before baptism the person receiving baptism turned to the west. In

---

25. Aghiorgoussis, "Meaning," 23.

the Greco-Roman culture the west, where the sun set, represented decline, destruction and death. Hades the realm of the dead also lay to the west. Facing the west, the baptisand renounced the Satan. The renunciation of Satan was coupled with a more plastic rite: the person spits towards the west. It is well-established custom for people to spit at persons or things they despise . . . after the renunciation of Satan the baptisand turned to the east, the place where the sun rises. The east is the direction of hope, life and light. He now bound himself with Christ, who is the Rising Sun. Neither the experience of the turning to the west or to the east, nor the gesture of spitting in contempt, which were so familiar to the Romans, can be found in our culture.[26]

Suppose that we, coming from our contemporary culture, were visiting an early church baptism session. Their practice could baffle us, though we owe them for passing down this tradition. One could easily criticize their practice as an example of syncretism. In some cultures, spitting in a church compound or during a Christian ritual would be taken as blasphemy. Though we share the same Bible and doctrine, their baptism practice looks different from the way we practice baptism in our cultures. The reason behind the difference is that the first-century believers were in a Roman superstitious context, as we are in the twenty-first century postmodern context. In the non-Western context, the emphasis on spiritual warfare and renouncing Satan makes perfect sense, but a Westerner who has a rationalistic worldview might find it difficult to connect. Another practice of baptism from the early churches in a different context may add to our understanding of how context sheds light on rituals:

In the Syrian churches, for example, the entire bodies of the catechumens were anointed with oil by the deacon or deaconess before baptism. This anointing was understood to bestow "the gift of the Spirit" before the actual baptism. Therefore, no laying on of hands occurred after the baptism. Some places gave the newly baptized members milk and honey after the ceremony to symbolize their spiritual entry into the "land of milk and honey," a name given in Scripture for Israel, itself a symbol for Christians of their own community.[27]

---

26. Lukken, *Rituals*, 159.
27. Ibid., 74.

As mentioned above, the Syrian church practice of giving milk and honey to the newly baptized members as a sign of blessing, in addition to the anointing of the oil, is something different from what we practice in our churches today. From the above two traditions, one can observe that culture influences the practice of rituals. As the believing community adjusts rituals, they add specific cultural details to the core meaning of the ritual. In the pastoralist areas of the southern Ethiopian tribes, there is always a shortage of water. People walk hours and hours to fetch water. As in the other highland areas, there are no rivers and streams flowing throughout the year. In the initiation rite of the Hamar people the initiate is buried in the sand to symbolize the cleansing of the person from all his childhood sins. In the traditional religion, the ritual was appropriate to the geographical environment, whereas Christianity refused to adopt it. Evangelical Christianity kept immersion as the model for baptism. Therefore, Christians have to create a little pond, which is difficult in the arid land, or wait until the rainy season comes.

As believing communities in other places contextualized baptism, the Hamar believers could have appropriated their ritual in a meaningful and relevant way without losing its biblical ground. In this case, burying the person in the sand could rightly signify dying and rising with Christ. It is theologically sound and culturally relevant. Meeks argues that the original mode of baptism, as Paul alluded to, was immersion, but for those persecuted Roman Christians in the catacombs the ideal approach was pouring water over the believers. He writes, "The earliest identifiable Christian meeting-house discovered by archaeologists, at Dura-Europos on the Euphrates, contained a basin that would hardly suffice for immersion. Perhaps the Pauline groups, too, had to adjust symbolism to physical necessity."[28] The physical limitation may have forced them to change the style of baptism as they hung on to the same meaning. Therefore, the focus was not on the mode of baptism but on the meaning of it and the message it conveyed.

Baptism is one of the rituals that intensify the journey of a disciple. It is not an end in itself, as some mistakenly think. In Anabaptist tradition baptism was taken as the beginning of a new era in the individual's life.

> A new convert of that period (16th c.) had requested baptism as an expression of his faith in Christ. When he came out of the water, he threw up his hands and shouted, "Praise God, it's all done," to

---

28. Meeks, *First Urban Christians*, 15.

which a wise pastor replied, "Oh no, my brother, it is not all done, it has only begun."[29]

Believers are not "all done" with baptism but they are empowered and embraced to continue the journey with the rest of the believing community. The problem with the "all done" understanding is that membership is taken as a one-time entrance into the Christian life, despite the possibility that the individual may drop out from the journey. The focus is on pre-baptismal interview performance and indoctrination which is often discontinued after the baptism. In such instances, the continual commitment and growth of the believer suffers a setback. Some desire to be members of the church for wrong reasons such as benefits and services.

Culture Change and Rituals

Rituals bond people, give new identity and bring transformation to the community. Tom Driver mentions three ways in which rituals are gifts to society; these are order, community and transformation.[30] These are great assets that help the community to live peacefully and orderly. The question is why Christian rituals have failed to bring order, community and transformation. If rituals are supposed to function that way, why are we experiencing disorder and disunity? Believers in Africa witness ethnic conflicts, genocide and corruption everywhere. Where are the Christian rituals? Why are they failing? Are they useless in the modern world? In a continent like Africa with a multitude of rituals, why is crisis rampant, and why are painful conflicts going without healing? Lukken rightly observes a few reasons why rituals are failing.

First, rituals have become more oriented to business rather than serving the community for better understanding of spiritual reality. The motives for performing rituals have more to do with economic benefit than with spiritual blessing or bonding. As a result, rituals lose their efficacy. When I asked my mother, who is in her nineties, to move with me to the city, she said, "Listen, if I die here in my village, people will come crying from different villages. I will be honored and respected by my friends and family. My casket will be carried slowly and it will be a wonderful farewell. But in the city your people are busy. No one will take my death seriously. They will rush my body to the graveyard and it ends just like that!" In today's world, rituals are performed

---

29. Schmidt, *Conversion*, 6.
30. Driver, *Magic*.

by professionals who have nothing to do with the community. Funerals are administered by funeral homes and weddings are prepared by wedding planners. Those were some of the rituals that brought people together and bonded them strongly. The role of the community has shifted from involvement to passive observation. Rituals are becoming means of income not means of community building.

When it comes to religious rituals, they are being commercialized too. Holidays like Christmas and Easter are becoming more about gifts than about Christ or the community. Churches are more concerned about members who can run the church well through their finances rather than discipleship and mission. Sacraments of the church such as baptism and Eucharist that are focused on Christ are fading away in Africa where new rituals motivated by business are taking over. Churches are selling anointed water, anointing oil and other anointed materials that distract people from following Christ to following spiritual celebrities.

The second issue regarding the ineffectiveness of rituals is that the role of the ritual experts is changing. The postmodern culture lifts those ritual experts to the level of celebrities and millionaires. The focus has shifted from the ritual and what it symbolizes to the expert and their spiritual tricks to get the attention of the crowds. Therefore, people look for the best experts in rituals of anointing and healings. The experts, on the other hand, experiment with new rituals to draw the attention of the society. In the continent of Africa, among many poor congregants, the prophets and apostles are millionaires. Where people struggle to get public transport, they enjoy private airplanes and the latest cars. Ritual experts were supposed to serve people and bring healing to the community. The team leadership of the church has been overtaken by a few charismatic individuals who can manipulate rituals to their own ends. That is not to deny the existence of genuine ministers and gifted men of God.

The third challenge related to rituals mentioned by Lukken is the expanding role of media in making people passive in the practice of rituals. The internet and television bring all rituals to public notice, wherever people are. But the side effect of the media's use of rituals is that it keeps people at a distance and unable to take part in the rituals. "Ritual consists of more than just seeing and hearing. Although all sorts of visual strategies can enhance the involvement of television viewers, they remain primarily spectators from outside. Participation in ritual via television is thus completely different from actual, physical participation."[31]

Currently many Christians choose to stay at home and watch Christian television rather than going to church and having an actual worship experience. They prefer to be entertained than to be involved. As Lukken rightly notes, viewing a service on television is different from being in the service and having a firsthand experience. Media on the one hand has brought rituals closer to people, but on the other hand has isolated people from involvement in rituals. The viewer may enjoy the service and receive teaching, but for true discipleship and ritual experience physical presence and face-to-face interaction is important.

The following diagram shows how rituals can be integrated in the spiritual journey of a believer. An individual has a context. He or she has background and an existing status. Then comes the transition period, where the individual converts or makes a decision to exit the old lifestyle. Through the process of mentoring the individual begins to experience the new life and is reintegrated into the community as a changed person. In Christianity the process of discipleship is crucial in integrating the individual to the church community and communion with Christ. Discipleship becomes a life time journey as the individual grows.

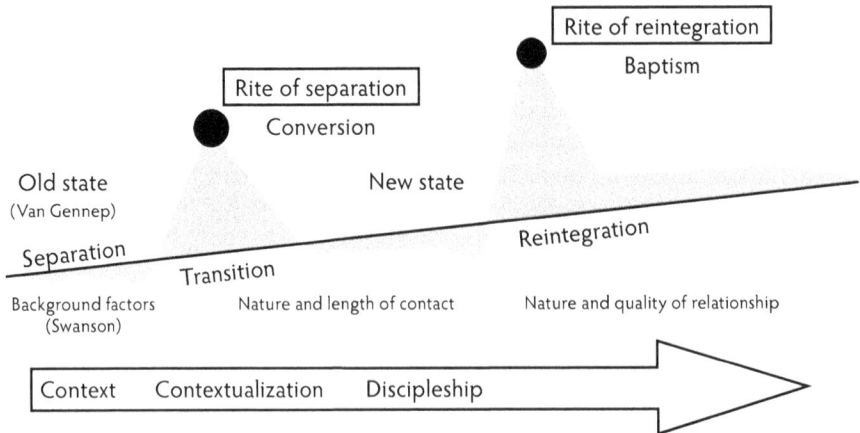

Figure 3. Contextualization of Rituals

---

31. Lukken, *Rituals*, 294.

Community: Seedbed of Discipleship

A believer who has entered the Christian life in conversion continues the discipleship journey in a community context. Christian identity formation takes place not in an isolated cave but in fellowship with other believers. It is the community that embraces a new convert into its fellowship and it is the community that confirms and approves the performance of the rituals by the convert. The spiritual journey of Christians is a journey of community. Though we are known by God as individual persons, our journey and our eternal destiny are communal, for whatever we do or do not do as Christians, we are responsible before God and before the family of God. Without meaningful connection with a community of God a believer will not grow spiritually strong. If a convert feels that he or she is not welcomed by the community, the chances of retreat are high.

Strong community ties help the convert to overcome the challenges and grow in faith. As Gordon Smith writes,

> Conversion takes place (1) when a person or group is connected to relationship in a religious community; (2) when rituals are enacted that foster experience and action consonant with religious mandate and goals; (3) when the rhetoric or system of interpretation of life is transformed into a religious frame of reference; and (4) when a person's role or sense of place and purpose is enacted and guided by religious sensibilities and structures.[32]

Relationship, rituals and involvement in the community are key factors in the conversion of individuals. One of the challenges for today's global Christianity is a lack of strong Christian communities that can withstand the pressure from the secular world. The individualistic Western culture poses a problem for communal life. It promotes independence, and the technology facilitates it. Privacy and personal preference is protected, and this affects the way people approach Christianity. The culture has turned Christianity from a communal religion to a private business.

> In the West conversion is easily thought of as an individual matter occurring in the interior (and solitary) life of the individual. Yet in a profound and mysterious way it may well be that the opposite

---

32. Smith, *Beginning Well*, 34.

is true: that conversion is derivative of the community. If this is
so, it is because the community is the mediator of conversion.[33]

The process by which a new believer is shaped and transformed into the
likeness of Christ takes place in a community that belongs to the kingdom
of God. The spiritual foundation of the community is important because
sometimes converts with passion, who are on fire for Christ, may lose their
zeal after encountering a community that has lost its purpose. In the village
where I grew up we have a cooking fire going early in the morning. The villagers
need each other. When there are no matches people who have fire willingly
share it with others. But in today's individualistic culture, rather than having
a conversation with fellow human beings, people hide behind their mobiles or
headphones, ignoring their fellow human beings. People are more influenced
by what is on the media than by their friends or families. As a result, people
turn out to be disciples of media and popular culture.

The current megachurch model that emphasizes the celebration dimension
of Christianity has also tended to make churches overlook the community
dimension of the church. Good music and entertainment has replaced
the accountability group where real lives are tested. Churches are more
concerned about the Sunday morning attendance, and neglect the community
transformation that has to take place during the week. The community aspect
of Christianity is getting less attention than ever. Smith is right when he writes,
"One of the most critical (and neglected) tasks in theological reflection on
conversion is appreciating the communal character of religious experience."[34]
Smith believes that both conversion and spiritual growth have a communal
character. Our need to respond to God individually cannot be ignored, but
decisions that are made can be strengthened by the community's support.
A new convert is born into a new family of God to be cared for and to be
accompanied in the discipleship process. As the modern culture separates
individuals from communities, believers lack a support system, and that
impedes their growth to maturity.

Though there is growth in membership of the churches in many parts
of the world, the key challenge is how to turn these converts into kingdom
communities with purpose and mission. Though people worship in the
same building and belong to the same denominational structure, there is
fragmentation of the body of Christ from many angles. Believers are not only

---

33. Ibid.
34. Ibid.

divided but also have a weak bond that can be easily broken when put under pressure. It is through the unity of the church that the church accomplishes its divine mission. Its calling is a calling to function in unity and its message is a message of unity.

In a world that is divided and full of hatred the church is expected to promote hope for peace and unity. The presence of the church as a community of love among the nations speaks a more powerful message than just a verbal proclamation. There may be different groupings or ethnic communities in the world but the church has to display a kingdom community. For instance, in African contexts there exist different Christian communities, but the problem is that their foundations are not always biblical. Believers take their ethnic identity more seriously than their identity in Christ. In the local churches one can easily observe ethnic communities within the larger community. When believers assemble under ethnic or racial identity within the umbrella of the church, it becomes an obstacle to the advancement of God's kingdom. The love that Christ has shown on the cross is unconditional, and is not based on our ethnic backgrounds or other qualities.

When African theologians propose the church as a family of God in Africa, my concern is that the concept has an exclusive nature, where the blood relationship comes before anything else. A clan member or a family member is always protected and others are treated as outsiders. The concept of family is so distorted that using it as a spiritual concept needs careful contextualization. A Christian community has a different set of values and structure than those of the traditional communities.

> The people of God, as a new community, have distinctive marks. This is a community of faith in Jesus Christ because it has developed from a 'covenant' which in itself is of divine origin. This covenant makes the Christian community a messianic community, a community that survives and lives through the support of her founder, Christ.[35]

In Africa the roots of all conflicts go deep in ethnocentrism and tribalism, where the insider gets all the privilege and others are devoid of their rights. The church is affected by what is going on in the society and church elections often are biased by ethnic connections. Africa has a communal culture that is commendable, but like all other human cultures it needs critical examination for all the pockets of evil hidden in the system. If the Christian community has

---

35. Onwubiko, *Church*, 67.

a different foundation than Christ, then the mission of the church is damaged rather than being promoted.

The global breakdown of community is exhibited in many forms. It begins in the smallest unit of the society – the family. Broken marriages and families lead to broken communities, which lead to all sorts of social and economic crises.

> The family, regarded as the basic bastion of stability in most cultures, is disintegrating in many parts of the world under the burden of poverty and migration of people from arid rural areas to monstrously overpopulated, slum-spawning megalopolises. In industrially developed countries, families are exploding serially under the pressure of modern life as they succumb to divorce, child neglect, domestic abuse, moral relativism, materialism and the loss of ideals.[36]

In the local churches broken relationships make people distrust each other. People with unhealed wounds find it difficult to open up and share their hearts. The discipleship process demands a genuine openness to connect with one another in order to transform lives. Too much pain and brokenness in the society make people put covers over their true identity and protect themselves from others. Children from abusive parents struggle to understand God as a father and others as brothers and sisters.

The question, then, is: if there is a critical community breakdown in different levels of the society, what has to be done to begin the mending? The church has to model community life for the rest of the world because healing comes from the finished work of Christ on the cross to save humanity. The foundational step is to understand the church as a community of God's kingdom. The church as described in the Scriptures is a family, the body of Christ, and the people of God. It is a community of called individuals for the purpose of spreading the gospel.

> The church is no mere collection of isolated individuals, but it has a corporate and communal nature which is absolutely essential to its true being. And finally, these truths show that being a community and a people is a gift from God through the work of Jesus Christ and the dwelling of the Holy Spirit.[37]

---

36. Snyder, *Community*, 46.
37. Ibid., 58.

The church is different from other social and political organizations in its purpose and origin. The church is not initiated by individuals, though they can contribute to the planting of churches; it is originated and headed by God. Understanding the church as a community of God's people emphasizes the priesthood of all believers and the need for connection through discipleship. Many people understand the church as an organization with stiff structures that resemble other human organizations.

> The New Testament presents to us an eclectic account of community formation because structures and orientation to life are secondary to the goal of a community, which is to live faithfully under the reign and rule of Christ until He returns. The New Testament does not present one model for the formation of the community called the church. Community formation, i.e. leadership structures and how the Christian life is expressed, is secondary to the focus of a community on the imminent return of the Lord Jesus Christ.[38]

The New Testament structure of the church centers on Christ, and believers work hand in hand according to their spiritual gifts. The principle is that the Christ-centered and gospel-based family of God works in perfect harmony to advance the kingdom of God. The New Testament presents principles not models. Leaders were appointed according to the discipleship structure that already existed in the church. The key problem of the church today is that the structure has become the overriding concern of the church, but the community formation is ignored. Leaders begin to believe that through the structure they can form a community, but it works the other way around. Communities with a common purpose and destiny form a structure to serve their purpose. I served as a district coordinator of spiritual ministries in the Ethiopian Kale Heywet Church in the south. My position was two administrative levels removed from the local church. Local churches report to the associational level and they report to the district office. Near to where I lived there is a local church that was going through chaotic conflict and fights that were not reported to us. As fellow believers, without waiting for a report, we showed up to talk to the church leaders regarding their situation. They confronted us asking, "Do you have an authorized letter to solve the problem? Who are you and what are you doing here?" Trying in vain to explain that the church is more than a structure, we were chased out of the church. When the church is stuck in structures and

---

38. Smith, "Missional Communities," 2.

loses its communal oneness it not only affects the spiritual growth of members but also its purpose for existence is lost.

The Need for Community

Community is what we are created for. It has a divine origin. Humanity is created to be in community and to enjoy one another. Adam's loneliness was not good before the Lord, so God brought Eve into his life. God created them man and woman so that they could be together, multiply and rule the creation. God created them to live, work, and fellowship with each other. Sin destroyed first the relationship between humanity and God, then all other relationships with fellow humans and the created world. The escalation of sin began in Adam's family, with Cain killing his brother Abel, and continued to grow worse. God in his sovereign eternal agenda created another community beginning with the family of Abraham.

The continuation of the people of God in the New Testament is the church, the body of Christ. It is a community created by God through Christ for the purpose of discipling the nations. The spiritual journey of believers is a long and tiring one that requires a community with one accord. It is the desire of humanity to enjoy the original intimacy that existed before sin. It is only through new creation in Christ that we can experience the original community as we are meant to. Kingdom community has a divine origin – it began with the Triune God. Bilezikian writes,

> One need go only three verses into the Bible to discover what is amply taught in the rest of Scripture, especially in the New Testament, that God is presented as a Tri-unity of divine entities existing as Father, Son, and Holy Spirit, the eternal community of oneness from whom all other communities derive life and meaning.[39]

A Christian community is different from other communities in that it has a different origin and a different set of values. It is the right remedy for the real needs of humanity. It answers the deep cry of humanity for connection and relationship. This Christian community is not a human fabrication; it has a divine origin that is founded on the Triune God, who is love. It is through this Christ-centered community that the people of God connect to one another

---

39. Bilezikien, *Community 101*, 17.

and work to link the world to the saving grace of God. God's people are called to serve as a community and to call people to this communal celebration and worship.

> When the church functions well as a human community, it provides a connecting link between God's renovating activity in the world and the needs of people . . . To view the church as a community of need is simply to admit that, unless the communication and celebration of the gospel are related to the needs of the people, life in the Christian church becomes sterile, routine, irrelevant, and very boring.[40]

If we consider the church as a community of God, then community formation is not an option. It is a divine mandate for Christians. Believers have to be intentional about forming a missional community for their own spiritual growth and ministry to the world. Though the postmodern culture is against communal life, and though capitalism spreads individualism, the church has no alternative but to be a community and to promote community. Discipleship happens and transforms people in a close communal interaction.

> The making of community may not be regarded as optional for Christians. It is a compelling and an irrevocable necessity, a binding divine mandate for all believers at all times. It is possible for humans to reject or alter God's commission for them to build community and to be in community. But this may happen only at the cost of forsaking the creator of community and of betraying his image in us.[41]

Ignoring community building diminishes the church's identity and mission. Unity is how the church functions as a body of Christ and where its mission is drawn from. Through genuine mentoring and building of community the church speaks to the world about true love and respect for humanity.

The most important service of community in Christianity is its provision of a venue for disciple making. To fulfill what Christ commanded the community of apostles before his ascension, the church needs a community of disciples and disciple makers. According to Jerome Murphy-O'Connor, sin made human beings inauthentic. Of course, lack of authenticity can be the biggest obstacle for the existence of community and its strong emphasis on relationship. Christ

---

40. Alston, *Church*, 69.
41. Bilezikian, *Community 101*, 27.

in his incarnation displayed authentic humanity. Murphy-O'Connor writes, "[Paul] saw the human situation as irredeemable from within but not from without. Hence, he consistently emphasizes that authenticity is made possible only through divine intervention, e.g. 'You who were dead . . . God has made alive' Col 2:13."[42]

To have a positive influence on the world around us believers need each other. We need each other to speak louder and to influence wider, as some groups of believers can accomplish more and reach many in communicating the gospel. An organized and unified move is more effective than the isolated efforts of individuals in mission.

> The community mediates Christ to the world. The word that he spoke is not in our contemporary world unless it is proclaimed by the community. The power that flowed forth from him in order to enable response is no longer effective unless manifested by the community. As God once acted through Christ, so he now acts (2 Cor 5:19–20) through those who are "conformed to the image of his son" . . . what Christ did in and for the world of his day through his physical presence, the community does in and for its world.[43]

Two key issues are mentioned by Murphy-O'Connor. First, the message is communicated and mediated in community. What we proclaim in words can only be authenticated by the demonstration of our life in the community. Second, our communal presence is a continuation of the ministry of Christ. The incarnate Christ was preaching the good news of the kingdom in words and deeds and the church as community has to extend the work Christ started. Without a strong community to energize and support the mission of the church our evangelism becomes ineffective.

> An increasing number of Christians are waking up to the fact that to a large extent the church has become ineffective in fulfilling its mission because it has lost a sense of its own identity as community. They realize that not every organization that calls itself a church represents the church as Christ conceived it . . . whereas the essential definition of the church is to be a community of oneness that unites God's people into one body, the church,

---

42. Murphy-O'Connor, *Becoming Human Together*, 142.

43. Ibid., 186.

after twenty centuries of existence, has to rediscover its own basic identity as community.[44]

Community formation is a process in which we learn how to be the best family of God in our specific contexts. Each cultural context begs for a different formulation of community, but the biblical foundation of community does not change. As twenty-first-century believers, we can learn from Scripture and the early church the principles of forming effective discipleship communities. Three lessons stand out: First, more than anything else (culture, tradition or race) Christian communities need a strong biblical foundation. Though there is not a biblical outline of steps, the Bible offers us principles which we can apply to our specific contexts. There is a long debate on what is the right biblical model of church structure: is it episcopal or congregational or hierarchical or missional, or what? Smith writes,

> . . . diverse forms of communities seeking after that same thing, to be conformed to Christ and faithfully live under His rule and reign awaiting His return. The New Testament structured and shaped the identities of the people of God while using cultural expressions to help them live faithfully under Christ's lordship.[45]

The structure is not the main issue for the early church; it is the foundation and the focus of the community. Structures were culturally conducive and facilitated the growth of disciples and the mission of the church. There are diverse structures in diverse cultures but the same foundation and the same purpose.

Regarding the practical steps, Smith outlines three examples of community formation in the early church that can be of help to us. These were households, associations and philosophical schools. First, the household structure was a basic building block of the society. "This structure, embedded in the daily lives of the culture, provided an accessible model for the church. The relationships of father, mother, children, slaves, workers, business associates, etc., all functioned within a household structure."[46] Second, associations were built on the model of the household but were extended into the community. These fostered close relationships based on ethnicity, work and living location. Such

---

44. Bilezikian, *Community 101*, 48.

45. Smith, "Missional Communities," 197.

46. Ibid.

associations were created formally and informally as people met for different social occasions.

> They consisted of food-related groups (such as fishermen, bakers, and farmers), potters and smiths, weavers, and builders (such as carpenters, stone cutters, and tent makers) . . . The second letter to the Thessalonians exemplifies this work, as does the letter to the Ephesians and various other letters.[47]

Today, work places, workout places, and worship places bring people together to form small communities. These social connections can serve to promote relationships between believers and provide opportunities for discipleship.

The third kind of communal structure in the first century was the philosophical school. These schools brought masters and disciples together. These structures were similar to our educational institutions but they went deeper in that they focused on moral and ethical formation rather than just passing on information. The education system was based on imitation that addressed the whole person.

> Philosophy was foremost a way of life in antiquity. Imitation is an important theme that runs throughout education and philosophy, Paul repeatedly employs imitation in many of his letters, including 1 Thessalonians. Imitation of a model, a person, was integral to learning. The Stoic philosopher Seneca also noted the importance of imitation.[48]

There are three lessons we can learn from the early church's contextualized approach to discipleship structure. First, the focus was not just on the conversion of the individual but on discipleship. People may join the church for different reasons, motivated by different needs. Believers must make sure that new converts begin their journey from the right position with right understanding.

Second, there was rigorous and contextually relevant instruction to mature the converts. The fact that there were three years of contextual instruction and follow-up shows how the early Christians took the discipleship process seriously. There was no rush to the pulpit as in the present-day quick-fix approach, no "I can do better than you" popularity contest, but quiet learning time to be shaped to the likeness of Christ. The training included intellectual,

---

47. Ibid., 198.
48. Ibid.

emotional and spiritual elements. Oral training, prayer and exorcism were included in the curriculum.

Finally, after going through the training process the baptism and post-baptismal rites followed. In a meaningful culmination of the ritual process, the converts dedicated themselves to the cause of Christ with understanding. Finn writes that "in the baptismal rebirth, in the communal kiss and embrace, and in the meal, the community was itself reborn and its family ties renewed. The rites by which new members were incorporated at once increased and regenerated the body of the faithful."[49] The addition of new members strengthened the community and brought freshness to the existing fellowship. It was a contextualized discipleship suited for the persecuted and rejected community of the early Christians. This was the mystery behind their success in the midst of hardship. Without armed conflict and political power they entered the palace and made the emperor Constantine submit himself to Christianity. They followed Christ faithfully and the influence of the church filled the environment as far as influencing the political arena.

A lesson from Celtic Christianity can also educate us today in our own attempts to form a community of disciples. The Celts received Christianity from the ministry of St Patrick and his contextualized approach in which he preached the gospel and also confronted the social evils. Celtic Christians formed a monastic community that was focused on transforming their world not running from it. Compared to the Roman institutionalized Christianity,

> the Celtic monastic communities produced a less individualistic and more community-oriented approach to the Christian life. This affected the way in which – in parish churches, communities, tribes, and families – the people supported each other, pulled together, prayed for each other, worked out their salvation together, and lived out the Christian life together.[50]

Because of its community-based purposeful Christianity this Celtic group was effective in their mission strategy. Their approach to mission was life-generated, Spirit-empowered and community-supported. George Hunter describes the influence of Celtic Christianity as follows: "Through several generations of sustained mission, Celtic Christianity thus re-evangelized Europe, helped bring Europe out of the dark ages, fueled Charlemagne's

---

49. Finn, "Ritual Process," 79.
50. Hunter, *Celtic Way*, 30.

Carolingian renaissance, and ushered in the 'Holy Roman Empire.'"[51] Discipleship-based mission not only has a tremendous impact on others but also has a power to break down the stronghold of the enemy.

The Celtic community not only facilitated growth of the believers but also opened the door for communal evangelism that made them effective in their mission to the world. Hunter mentions a few ways in which the Celts communicated the gospel, by both being and doing. First, they practiced group evangelism. "Christians usually evangelized as a team – by relating to the people settlement; identifying with people; engaging in friendship, conversation, ministry, and witness – with the goal of raising up a church in measurable time."[52] Second, they lived with depth, compassion and power in mission. Third, they focused on imaginative prayer. Finally, they emphasized the role of community in the process of conversion. Their Christ-centered life and prayer-backed mission helped the community-owned Celtic church glorify God and extend his kingdom. Compared to the traditional way of doing mission – beginning with the presentation of the gospel, followed by conversion and incorporation of the convert – the Celtic way is different because the community comes first, then conversation that leads to genuine conversion. According to their approach evangelism is about helping people to belong so that they can believe.[53]

The need for community, both for our survival in this evil world and for our mission as a people of God, is a key lesson that we can derive from Celtic Christianity. The body of Christ lives, grows, and witnesses together as a community. The effective spread of the gospel by both first-century believers and Celtic Christians issued from their communal journey of discipleship. The contemporary church must adopt this model. Biblical contextualization is crucial for the effectiveness of the church's mission.

---

51. Ibid., 40.
52. Ibid., 47.
53. For more detailed discussion, see ibid.

5

Reflection on the Ethiopian Evangelical Context

Though discipleship is a global church issue, as I have discussed above, it would also be helpful to give a specific example. I would like to reflect on the discipleship journey of Ethiopian evangelical churches. The discussion will include the challenges, the opportunities and prospects of evangelical churches in their historical and contemporary contexts. I am choosing Ethiopia primarily because it is my immediate context, but also because it is one of the fastest growing churches in Africa. It is the second most populated country in Africa, inhabited by close to one hundred million people.

Ethiopia, mentioned in the Bible several times and one of the early recipients of the gospel, has a rich tradition of ancient churches and involvement in mission. The Ethiopian Orthodox Church, to which 40 percent of the population adheres, needs a thorough discussion, but that is beyond the scope of this book. However, the discipleship issue is probably the main reason why the Ethiopian Orthodox Church has lost its spiritual cutting edge and has turned to observance of tradition and culture rather than biblical spirituality and meaningful worship. Though the Ethiopian Orthodox Church has much positive tradition, discipleship and mission have not been the strength of the church. This study limits its scope to the one hundred years of activity of evangelical churches in Ethiopia. Without going into details, it will highlight some of the integration issues in contextualization and discipleship in relation to the history and contemporary context of the church.

Historical Background of Ethiopian Evangelical Churches

Ethiopian evangelical Christianity is now over a century old and has gone through a series of persecutions that have shaped the spiritual journey of the church. After years of hardship and persecution, for the last three decades the evangelical church is experiencing relative freedom of worship and is sharing its faith with others. It is still one of the fastest growing and vibrant churches in Africa, but is struggling with discipleship issues, as is the case in other global churches. As the number of believers has increased, the impact of the church on the community should be expected to increase, but that is not the case. The respect of the community for the churches is evaporating because of the ethical and moral failure of believers. The denominations are struggling to keep the unity of the churches and many young people are leaving the mainline mission churches for newly planted churches. As internal issues distract the churches, the mission of reaching others is facing a setback. Today there are a significant number of unreached people groups in the border and Muslim areas of Ethiopia. There are still thirty-three unreached people groups, totaling about twenty-four million people, who have yet to hear the gospel. Many surrounding nations are considered to be mainly unreached as well.[1] To understand this lack of discipleship and its consequences it is good to begin with an analysis of the historical background of the evangelical churches in Ethiopia.

Though Christianity came to Ethiopia earlier than it did to many sub-Saharan African countries, around the fourth century AD, its growth and expansion has been confined because of internal political struggles and lack of continuous discipleship and biblical teaching. The first recipients of Christianity in Ethiopia were the royal family, and from there Christianity began its spread from top down. Converts at times were forced to become Christians as the king advanced his territories to the south from his northern stronghold. Mass evangelism with mass baptism was the methodology used by Ethiopian Orthodox churches for many centuries. Many adherents of the faith practiced their traditional religion freely and claimed to be Christians. At the end of the nineteenth century missionaries began their work in Ethiopia mainly to revive the existing church. The evangelical churches grew fast in the twentieth century and took their own identity by separating from the Orthodox church. My intention is to write a history of the evangelical church and its mission, but I would like to highlight the historical contexts of the discipleship journey of the church in relation to its current struggles and challenges.

---

1. Urga et al., "Ethiopian."

The Ethiopian evangelical church has three streams of tradition that came together as an evangelical church movement. The first is the Lutheran mission stream in northern and western Ethiopia. The missionaries from Sweden (SEM) and other European countries (NLM, GHM) began their mission work in northern Ethiopia (Eritrea) and extended the work to the Oromo people of western Ethiopia. Today Wellega is the stronghold of the Mekane Yesus Church and the majority of the national denominational leaders are from this region.

The second stream is the SIM missionary work in southern Ethiopia, that started in 1928. The southern people groups are diverse in ethnic background and the Ethiopian Kale Heywet Church is strong in the southland. The third stream is the central and urban Pentecostal movement that had its beginnings right before the Marxists took over the country. The Mennonites in the east and the Full Gospel churches in the capital are the fruits of this movement. It is more indigenous than missionary-influenced when it comes to its leadership structure and organizational model. The above three streams contributed to today's evangelical church in Ethiopia. Ethiopian evangelicals today, despite their different traditions and doctrinal inclinations, resemble each other in their worship style and spiritual understanding.

Western Ethiopian Stream

For proper understanding of the discipleship issues in the church, it is good to consider the social context of the people and the planting of the churches. The ways in which the gospel was integrated with the social context, and how that affected the lives of believers, reveals the strengths and weaknesses of the discipleship ministry. Though the missionary work of the SEM began in Eritrea, the vision was to reach the Oromo of western and central Ethiopia. Therefore, I would like to focus on the social context of western Ethiopia.

The Social Context of the West

Since the unification strategy of Emperor Menelik II the relationship between the central government and the people in the periphery has not been good. Many communities in the periphery acquired a negative attitude towards the center. The western Oromo people, like the other peoples in the south, experienced extreme humiliation and subjugation by the central government. They were disadvantaged in the following areas. First, economically, they were exploited by the landlords from the central government and forced to fund the abusive administrative system. Oyvind Eide writes,

> They were reduced to cash-crop producers, exploited to the limit of their capacity in order to provide the financial means necessary to sustain the dominating structure. As a result, they were enclosed individually in [a] relationship of subordination to their landlords, without any possibility of applying for relief to the administration or to legal authorities, leaving them exposed and prone to legal abuse. For peasants the basic experience of life in the beginning of the 1970s was therefore subjugation and humiliation, a day-to-day battle for sheer survival.[2]

This humiliation, abuse and domination is the experience that continues to haunt the lives of the people, and its scars continue to influence them and their relationships with others.

Second, related to the first, the disintegration of the cultural system, caused by the domination of the central government, affected the social identity of the people. One of the worst things that happened to the people in the periphery was an identity crisis. The breakdown of the cultural structure with the domination of the people from the central government has created a great void in the lives of the peripheral people which Christianity filled later. This breakdown affected the people psychologically, socially and economically. Eide writes,

> For the Wallaga region in the western periphery, integration into the empire proved to be the turning point in history. Orthodox Christianity, arriving on the arena as a part of the new order, represented a powerful challenge to traditional Oromo religion. The effect on the Oromo societies in the region was dramatic, as political, social and cultural tradition of the different groups broke down.[3]

Third, *Afaan Oromiffa*, the language of the Oromo, was rejected as an official language of the district and was replaced by Amharic, the language of the central government. In the name of the unification of the country the languages of the people in the periphery were ignored.

---

2. Eide, *Revolution*, 86.
3. Ibid., 23.

[Afaan] Oromo was denied any official status and it was not permissible to publish, preach, teach or broadcast in Oromo. In court or before an official an Oromo had to speak Amharic or use an interpreter. Even a case between Oromos, before an Oromo speaking magistrate, had to be heard in Amharic. I sat through a mission service at which the preacher and all the congregation were Oromo but at which the sermon as well as the service was given first in Amharic, which few of the congregation understood at all, and then translated into Oromo. The farce had to be played out in case a Judas informed and the district officer fined or imprisoned the preacher.[4]

Being forced to speak a different language and defend their rights in court in a language different than their mother tongue, even in their own village and town, devastated their confidence. Despite the government rules, the missionaries encouraged the translation of the Bible into Afaan Oromo and made efforts to translate their preaching.

The Lutheran Mission Work

The root of evangelical mission in Ethiopia goes further back into the seventeenth century with the coming of the German Lutheran Mission, but because of the political situation in the country it was difficult to make a significant impact, and their work experienced many interruptions and setbacks. Mission work with greater continuity was begun in northern Ethiopia by the Swedish Evangelical Mission in 1866 in a place called Hamassein. According to Eshete, "the vision of establishing mission work, particularly with the Hamassein priests, had been born as a secondary goal when the political situation in Ethiopia hampered them from reaching the Oromo areas."[5] The missionaries primary vision was to go to the western part of Ethiopia to evangelize the Oromo; this was a passion inherited from earlier missionaries' writings. They patiently waited in preparing for the work by training Oromo ex-slaves until the door was open. In the meantime, they opened schools to teach local priests and indigenous people.

In 1904, Onesimus, an Oromo ex-slave and one of the few missionary converts, arrived in Wellega in western Ethiopia with two former Orthodox

---

4. Hussein, "Politics of Language," 36–37.
5. Eshete, *Evangelical Movement*, 71.

priests to start the missionary work. Because of the existence of the Ethiopian Orthodox Church in the area, they began working with the existing church. Their desire was to revitalize the church through teaching the Bible and focusing on Jesus for the salvation of souls. After trying to work with the Orthodox church for some time, the differences became obvious, and when they were pushed out of the church they began their own congregation.

> When the children of evangelical believers were no longer baptized in the Orthodox church, and when the local priests refused to officiate at the funerals of Bible readers, there is no other way but to look for new possibilities and structures to worship God, to receive the sacraments and have the dead buried in a Christian way.[6]

In other words, their dreams to reform the Ethiopian Orthodox Church ended. Their ministry moved from renewal to separate development because of rejection by the Ethiopian Orthodox Church. The evangelicals finally decided to disconnect themselves from the church they wanted to reform.

Conversion, Ritual and Community

What we can observe from the beginning of the Ethiopian Evangelical Church Mekane Yesus (EECMY) in the west is that it is led by mainly indigenous evangelists with the support of foreign missionaries. Onesimus, one of the key leaders, translated the Bible into *Oromiffa*, which helped the converts to hear the message in their own language. At the beginning, the attempt was to reform the existing Orthodox church rather than to call people to conversion. The missionaries accepted the baptism of the Ethiopian Orthodox Church as a true baptism whereas other evangelical churches rejected it. The new converts' decisions were perceived as a continuation of their former understanding rather than a new beginning. Because of the socio-political crisis, the preaching of the good news was received well by the local people, but it was not only the contextual pressure but also the presentation of the gospel in the vernacular language that motivated the locals to join the evangelical church. The use of vernacular language in the oral communities made the church successful not only in Ethiopia but also in the continent of Africa in general. Eshete notes,

---

6. Launhardt, *Evangelicals in Addis Ababa*, 114–115.

The Bible in their hands and in their own vernacular languages provided the basis for new spiritual insights and interpretations that were communicated far and wide in indigenous forms to a large illiterate community. African preachers appropriated and nuanced biblical instruction for the level and condition of their local audience.[7]

This approach not only opened up the hearts of the people to listen to the good news but also lifted up the identity of the people as they heard God speaking to them in their own tongue.

Though the message was communicated in the vernacular language, there were issues in other areas of contextualization and discipleship. Let me mention some: First, there was a lack of contextualization of theological ideas in the process of integration with Christianity. In any cultural or religious context, it is very important to critically examine the ideas of the traditional religion before they are incorporated into Christianity. A non-critical approach to cultural ideas and a lack of spiritual discernment in incorporating traditional customs can hinder the growth and maturity of believers. In the Western stream of Christianity lack of critical contextualization could be taken as a major contributor to the discipleship crisis surfacing today. To illustrate, Eide discusses the idea of sin among the western Oromo converts. From the traditional Oromo perspective, he writes that "the concept of sin was traditionally related to *safuu*, the rights and duties between individual and group, the law of the world order and the social order as given to them by *Waaqa* from the beginning."[8] In other words, sin is what the community rejects as cultural abnormality. Sin, which is important to Christian conversion and theology, took on a different cultural meaning. A pastor from Wellaga district witnessed,

> What you see is to a large extent the elders practicing their Oromo interpretation of *cubbuu*. Remember we are first-generation Christians. Christianity is still on the surface. Underneath you find culture and religion deep, deep down. Biblical ethics, as interpreted by the missionaries, have only modified our old practices, not changed them.[9]

---

7. Eshete, *Evangelical Movement*, 128.

8. Eide, *Revolution*, 75.

9. Ibid., 76.

Such an understanding categorizes sin and its punishment on a different level, as dictated by the culture, and not according to Scripture. Believers care more for the opinion of the community than the judgment of God. Separation from the community due to wrong action scares people more than their eternal separation from God. As the next generation continues to build upon such a foundation, it is obvious how believers can depart further from the biblical concept and meaning of sin. This is just one example, but other similar issues can be mentioned that are incorporated without critical assessment.

Instead of re-baptizing the Orthodox converts, the missionaries instituted the initiation ritual of confirmation. The attempt to work with the Orthodox church had its own influence on the evangelical believers. The attitude of the western Oromo evangelicals towards rituals is closer to the traditional Orthodox understanding than the evangelical sacramental theology. For instance, Eide writes, "Communion was followed by remarkable high church attendance (91 percent). When questioned on their interpretation of Holy Communion, the majority (22 percent) of communicant members gave the most interesting answer that 'it gives eternal life.'"[10] Such understanding is not an evangelical teaching but rather is adopted from the Ethiopian Orthodox liturgy and doctrine.

Among the Ethiopian Orthodox Church followers, Eucharist is special. It is an area where the church leadership plays its power game, because without them there are no sacraments. Rituals, rather than serving to point to Christ, serve the interests of the leaders, though this is also manifested in the evangelical congregations. Eide writes, "Keeping in mind the elevated interpretation of Holy Communion, and the fact that only pastors can administer this sacrament, help us to bring the position and power of the evangelical pastors into focus."[11] In many traditional Ethiopian cultures, the leader is respected and honored as a special divinely appointed person. The early believers' understanding of rituals gave the leaders an elevated status that contradicted the Lutheran theology of the priesthood of all believers.

Second, evangelical Christianity in the west of Ethiopia failed to address the identity issue – that is, ethnic identity versus identity in Christ. This issue has continued to influence Western evangelical Christians in their discipleship journey to this day. In the beginning, the motivation for conversion to

10. Ibid., 79. Eide is not clear about the majority of the 22% but his point is the dominance of Ethiopian Orthodox Theology on the converts rather than the position of missionaries or the teaching of the Scripture.

11. Ibid., 80.

Christianity was resistance to the domination of the central Amhara regime and their type of Christianity.

> It seems clear that the change of belief system towards the evangelical faith in the western periphery came about as a result of conscious dissociation from central elements in the religious past of the people. In this respect, the dissociation from the religion of the ruling Amhara elite is of a particular interest to note. It therefore seems reasonable to interpret the growth of the evangelical movement at the periphery in part as a reaction or an expression of cultural resistance against domination and exploitation by the Amhara political and religious center.[12]

Christianity became a unifying factor in the revolt against the domination of the existing central government. Christianity, in uplifting the dignity of people and respecting the language used as a media of communication, played a crucial role in solidifying the unity and identity of the people in western Ethiopia. Many people joined the church not only for the good news of the gospel but also for the embracive and uplifting nature of Christianity. It is common in history for people to have various motives for attending church; through discipleship, those attitudes and motives can be transformed, refocused and reshaped. Rather than contextualizing the gospel in discipling the converts, the missionaries were devoted to passing on the Lutheran tradition from their own context with its forms, policies and organizational structures. The lack of close discipleship was revealed during the invasion of the Italians, as J. Bakke reports:

> At the time they [the missionaries] were expelled none of them had been able to establish a fully indigenous work. They had not ordained any pastor and one of the missions had not even employed a single evangelist. The evangelical groups found themselves deserted and without an ordained minister to shepherd their flocks.[13]

One might raise several questions: Why did the missionaries fail to ordain? Were there no capable converts to lead the churches? In all these years what was the task of missionaries if they did not have people to replace them? The calling of a missionary is to make disciples. Discipleship is equipping others to

12. Ibid., 92.
13. Bakke, *Christian Ministry*, 136.

lead and serve others. Sowing the seed of the gospel is one thing, but watering it and enabling it to bear living fruit is another thing, which the missionaries failed to accomplish.

The external pressure from the central government brought people of the western region together. With Christianity, the ethnic bonds found additional strength and were firmly cemented. In the process, the more inclusive kingdom community concept was weakened because of the narrowed identity markers.

> The church exists in a society as a community of disciples whose faith in the God of Jesus Christ assumes historical form in word and sacrament, living and worshipping, personal and structural relationships. It is within historical society that it exists and carries out its saving mission. Yet it also stands over against society, irreducible to it, challenging it, even judging it, in the world but not finally of it.[14]

Whatever narrative we inherit as a society, the church always challenges and judges the narrative in the light of the kingdom of God and its eternal mission. Here is the place for contextualization – helping the community to keep the tension balanced between indigenization and the pilgrim principle in which a Christian operates as a dual citizen. Once the church is reduced to operate within certain ethic and racial confines, the mission of the church is also confined.

Third, related to the other issues, the political involvement of the EECMY is rooted in its response to the historical context that addresses both the social and spiritual needs of the people. EECMY is one of the denominations in Ethiopia that are actively involved in politics, and it voices its concern when there is injustice. It is an appropriate approach because a disciple is called to be involved in the community. However, it has to be done in a balanced way for the glory of God and the benefit of the community. In Ethiopian evangelical church history, with little involvement in politics by believers, it is difficult to evaluate the contribution of churches. Yet the EECMY has made a significant contribution through its influence on the top leadership in Ethiopian politics. In a context like Africa, political involvement takes wisdom, soul searching, discernment and boldness, which is part of a continual journey of discipleship. "Basically there is no doubt that the aim of the Mekane Yesus Church was to

---

14. McDonagh, *Church and Politics*, 34.

give witness to Christ and to serve fellow men in need. But, as we have seen, the church by its sheer existence was drawn into the political realm."[15]

The training of believers should give them opportunities and a platform to be involved in the political realm, but it has been a difficult ground so far to exhibit Christ-like character in the complex political arena. It is an area that needs more research and study to understand how far to involve oneself in politics as a believer, especially when there is a huge risk as is the case in Africa. The EECMY is one of the prominent examples of a church involved in politics, in a constructive way. The discipleship issues in the evangelical churches of western Ethiopia can be summed up partly as an identity-related lack of critical contextualization and lack of focus in community involvement. These are a few examples of how contextualization and discipleship can mature the church and equip it for mission, and of how lack of integration can negatively affect the journey of the church as a community of disciples.

The Southern Ethiopia Stream

The southern region of Ethiopia is a peripheral area that has had an experience similar to that of the western and other areas. The southern region is more diverse in language and in culture than the west. Lutheran missionaries mainly from Europe evangelized the western region, but the southern region was worked by a mix of Presbyterian, Baptist and interdenominational missionaries from the United States and Canada. Southern Ethiopia as a region experienced more peace and economic progress through the introduction of the gospel than any other region. For instance, among the southwestern tribes there had been continuous conflict, and that was significantly reduced by the introduction of the gospel. Currently, the majority of the educated political leaders are either Christians or have been influenced by Christian presence in the area. But one question remains: Why is corruption and injustice still an issue in the region? Where are the disciples of Christ and what role are they playing in the community?

Social Context of the South

Southern Ethiopia was structured under a traditional administrative system of chiefdoms until the unification (some call it "colonization") agenda of

---

15. Ibid., 92.

Emperor Menelik II (1889–1909). Through his army he took control of the south and he also established a *gabbar*[16] tax system which became a burden to the southerners. Not only did he introduce a new oppressive system but he also destroyed the existing traditional structures. After losing their administrative system, and being controlled by the central government with a new national language, things in the south went out of control. "They had their own cultural, political and economic system and they did not acknowledge any central political power which was dominating them."[17] Though they were forced to accept it and function under the new system, it affected their self-identity and communal lifestyle. Burdened by these new systems of administration and also by fear of the evil powers through the witchdoctors, southern Ethiopia was in a depressing situation when the missionaries arrived.

There were also traditional prophets or witchdoctors teaching new ethical laws and promising the coming of a new era led by new people. Esa of Wolaitta is a prime example: Paul Balisky writes that Esa was a "John the Baptist of the Omotic population of southern Ethiopia. He expanded the limited cosmology of the Wolaitta so that entire families could freely and openly worship *Tosa*."[18] The content of the message was more ethical guidance and rejection of demonic worship and traditional practices. Around the same time the Aari people, further south, also had such a message circulated throughout the villages, known as *Aket Kal*, literally meaning "word of ancestors." It was similar to what Esa was teaching in Wolaitta. How those messages and individuals were connected or separated needs thorough research which is not the intent of this book.

In short, cornered in life from all angles, many lived and died without a foreseeable future of hope. Oppressed by the political system, abused by the religious leaders and having lost their identity in the existing social crisis, the southern people could only wait for a restoration and deliverance from someone or somewhere. It was at such a time that the missionaries came to the south with the good news. The context was pregnant for change and transformation. The southerners were happy to receive missionaries, except

---

16. According to Tolo, the word "*gabbar*" literally could be translated "tribute giver." The local peasant or the *gabbar* was "one who had to pay tribute." The tenants in the southern periphery were forced to pay tribute or tax to the new landowners (Tolo, *Sidama and Ethiopian*, 72).

17. Ibid., 65.

18. Balisky, *Wolaitta Evangelists*, 106.

for some pockets of resistance from the adherents of the Ethiopian Orthodox Church. Dena Freeman correctly summarizes the context:

> The story of Wolaitta conversion thus centers around the breakdown of a traditional politico-ritual system under the pressure of conquest and colonialism. The resulting spiritual void, and the attendant feelings of humiliation and suffering, left people open to new religious ideas and receptive to the messages of foreign missionaries who happened to arrive at the time.[19]

The multiple crises of the southern Ethiopian community – social, political, economic and structural – motivated them to search for new life and new experience. The theory that crisis leads to conversion happens to be true in the context of the southern people. "The empirical research of the early pioneers in the field of psychology of religion suggests that religious conversion often occurs during and after a period of stress, despair and even crisis."[20] The crisis was so deep and painful that many converts were willing to pay whatever cost for their newfound faith in Christ. After the treatment they had suffered under the rulers and the fear of spirits that had paralyzed them for years, it was unthinkable to relapse and practice the traditional religion. The motivating factors for those southern rural communities to join the church were the message of the gospel that gave freedom, the love of new believers for one another, and the new identity that the new fellowship brought to the community.

The simple and understandable presentation of the gospel by the local evangelists was attractive and appealing. There is an often-told story about the evangelists: one of the evangelists went to a new area, climbed a tree and began screaming. The villagers were shocked by the man's action and gathered to watch what was going on. He continued screaming until crowds gathered around the tree. As soon as he saw a large crowd around him, he came down from the tree and began preaching the gospel. The villagers were amazed by the message and replied, So what shall we do? He told them to repent and come to Christ, and later on they planted a church in that village. The first generation of believers always compared their life before Christ with their freedom in Christ, which made them always thankful.

---

19. Freeman, "Pentecostalism," 234.
20. Kim, *Understanding*, 20.

SIM Missionary Work

The SIM, formerly Sudan Interior Mission, now Serving in Mission, has a vision for advancing the kingdom of God from the coastal areas of Africa to the unreached places in the interior of Africa. SIM started its ministry in southern Ethiopia in 1927. The SIM missionaries were strong on preaching Christ, focusing on Scripture and behavioral transformation. Moreover, their missionary approach was based on the urgency for mission, as emphasized at the Edinburgh 1910 mission conference, and "the three self" principle. The church planted by SIM in Ethiopia is the Ethiopian Kale Heywet Church, one of the largest denominations in Ethiopia. Currently the denomination has more than eight million members. The SIM missionaries faced difficulty in getting permission for missionary work due to opposition from the priests of the Ethiopian Orthodox Church and the majority of the political leaders.

Though the king's modernizing policy favored them, it was not easy to legally preach the gospel. Part of the reluctance in allowing the missionaries into the south was the realization that the south was a pagan territory different from the Christian north. As they continued to wait for official permission, with the recommendation of one of the officials they took a break and planned to travel to Jimma, the place in which they wanted to start their missionary work. According to Balisky, the guides chose to lead them through Kullo Konta, but on their way Dr Lambie met his former friends who contributed to his settlement before they reached their destination.[21] Others think that, though the guides missed the route, it was divine guidance that changed their direction so that they began their work among the southern people. Later, after scouting the surrounding regions, the missionaries decided to establish stations at three locations, namely Hossana, Wolaitta and Sidama. Through the ministry of the missionaries, churches were planted and the gospel spread quickly. After the planting of these churches there was a series of persecutions.

One of the amazing stories of the church in the south is its survival in the persecution of the Italian invaders. There is a difference among historians regarding the number of believers at the time of the missionaries' departure. The estimation is between forty-eight and one hundred believers. According to these numbers it seems that every year about four to ten believers had been added to the new movement. It is significantly low for a context seemingly ready for the coming of the missionaries. Then the astonishing fact is the growth of the church during the Italian invasion. In the years after the missionaries

---

21. Balisky, *Wolaitta Evangelists*.

were expelled, from 1937 to 1941 the church grew to 25,000 believers in two hundred local churches.[22] This shows that an average of 6,000 people came to Christ every year. The gap between ten people a year and 6,000 people is puzzling for many historians. The prophets of the traditional religion had predicted the coming of missionaries with a new message, and the social crisis was an opportune time to bring to Christ thousands who had been missed by the missionaries.

Conversion, Rituals and Community

Brian Fargher's book *The Origin of the New Churches Movement in Southern Ethiopia* is so far the most detailed and balanced history of the beginnings of the Ethiopian Kale Heywet Church in Southern Ethiopia. The three key issues discussed by Fargher are crucial for the discipleship journey of the churches. These are conversion, communication of sacraments and rituals, and community formation. In cross-cultural communication of the gospel or church planting, the initial stage of people's response, the process of establishing rituals without being misunderstood, and the formation of a community with scriptural values are keys to the maturity of the church. True discipleship can only flourish with good foundational decisions, holistic communication and strong Christ-centered community.

First, the missionaries and the indigenous people had some differences in their understanding of conversion. Let me give a few examples: the missionaries preached Bible-based sermons on the grace of God. For the oral people of the south who struggled with the fear of witchcraft, it was the power of God that was more attractive. Therefore, when someone made a decision, the assumptions of the missionaries and the indigenous people were often different. The interest and motives of the indigenous people were not congruent with the expectation and preaching of the missionaries. Fargher writes,

> The society in which they preached was largely illiterate, but the missionaries still emphasized that their message was based on the Bible. This approach had the potential failure because the listeners were unable to read the Book, the source of the authority . . . Even though much evangelistic preaching in the missionaries'

---

22. Cotterell, *Born at Midnight*, 102.

homeland emphasized God's mercy Ethiopians were much more concerned about his power.[23]

This mismatch of expectation between the converts and missionaries contributed to the nominalism that the church is experiencing today. The missionaries' intellectual approach to Christianity, without considering the power issues in the context, left a void that believers tried to fill in different ways.

Second, as Fargher notes, because of their background the SIM missionaries who worked in southern Ethiopia were conversion-centered. Conversion according to the missionaries was primarily a detachment of an individual or a group from their cultural rituals and customs. Of course, some of those cultural practices were against humanity and the Word of God. Therefore, the missionaries declared war against the devil that was largely hidden in the culture. As a result, conversion was a move away from the local culture to Christ and to Western culture. In preparation for baptism converts were expected to exhibit detachment from all their connections and associations with culture and tradition.

The reason for such an approach was based on the missionaries' emphasis on behavioral change. These expected behavioral changes to practices like drinking and polygamy were mainly external and observable. Many of the expectations were based on the missionaries' own cultural standards rather than biblical or contextual norms. The question "What does it mean to be a disciple of Christ in the context where I am living?" was not handled well. The converts struggled to live up to the expected standard and in some cases lived a double life – public and private. Of course the missionaries were reflecting and practicing the understanding of the time. Fargher adds,

> They were taught that separation was an integral part of true Christianity. It was as much part of their belief system as was conversion and the independent church. The missionaries passed this teaching on to their converts because they believed it was an essential part of their message.[24]

Henry Schmidt writes that a major pitfall is "measuring conversion by verbal declaration rather than by a new relationship towards God and mankind as evidenced by changed attitudes, goals and lifestyle."[25] In the southern

---

23. Fargher, *Origin*, 130.

24. Ibid., 29.

25. Schmidt, *Conversion*, 11.

Ethiopian case, external behavior was taken as evidence for true conversion. Converts were judged by what they did or did not do. They were expected to demonstrate their change externally. The result was conforming to others but not growing as followers of Christ. It is wonderfully put by Lane Adams in an analogy for conversion: "Conversion is like an invasion and the Christian life is like a war. There is a sincere but a mistaken form of evangelism today which gives the impression that the total conquest of the island is accomplished by the mere invasion."[26] The invasion is successful as thousands flock to the churches but the key issue of establishing the kingdom of God in the lives of people is often the missing piece.

Third, the initial responses of the converts were not congruent with what the missionaries were expecting. In revival meetings in the Western contexts people show their emotions and confess their convictions. In the oral and rural context of southern Ethiopia people were cold at the preaching of the gospel and less excited when they decided to follow Christ. The SIM missionaries observed and probably wondered why "conversions were not accompanied by tears and confessions." Probably the converts had no idea what they were entering into and what it would cost them at the end. In the traditional religion no one is sure about what is going to happen to that individual's life. You always wait and see. So for many in the south, conversion is a time to show in advance their willingness to learn more and to discover. I concur with Fargher: "Had these SIM evangelists taken time to examine in details the milieu in which they worked they might have considered their conviction unrealistic."[27]

Related to the above, the missionaries were always hesitant about the readiness of the believers for baptism. Of course, coming from different denominational traditions, the missionaries debated among themselves about when to baptize a convert. Fargher writes:

> There was a tension between the interpretation of baptism as an initiation rite and as a forward step in the convert's Christian faith experience. The two interpretations did not have much in common . . . It may be that the insistence on closed membership, and the necessity of the transition rite of baptism by immersion, was attributed to the pressure of the converts themselves.[28]

---

26. Adams, *Incredible Patience of God*, 25.
27. Fargher, *Origin*, 27.
28. Ibid., 144.

The role of rituals in the lives of traditional people was underestimated by the missionaries. Some converts were disappointed by the time of waiting to be baptized and to become full members of the community. In preparation for baptism the missionaries put together "believers' classes" that were neither attractive nor effective in a rural illiterate community. For instance, in 1936 in Jimma, from about seventy-five church attendees only ten to fifteen[29] were taking the believers' class. Discipleship and Christian training should fit the context and use contextually appropriate methods. In a majority oral community where stories and discussions are the media of communication, the Western way of classroom instruction and training focused on written material is unfitting to the setting. In a context where informal and on-the-job training is the custom, the intellectual focus has failed to bring real changes.

Discipleship materials, including Scripture in the native languages, were unavailable. To disciple converts the Scripture (the Word of God) has to take center stage. It is the Word of God that can shape and transform converts so that they can be disciples of Christ. SIM as a mission in Ethiopia was not actively involved in Bible translation, though there were attempts here and there. Probably the missionaries themselves were not sure about the use of language because Amharic was neither spoken by the majority of the southern people nor used in traditional worship. Though it was imposed by the government none of the southern ethnic groups used Amharic as their daily communication medium.

For the first converts who were expected to train others there were no materials available to use. The many different languages of southern Ethiopian became an obstacle to producing materials for discipleship programs. Fargher writes,

> The heavy emphasis of the mission on evangelism *per se* meant that linguistics were often moved from one area to another; the result was that the quantity of linguistic materials they prepared was disappointingly small. These pioneers left an example rather than a great deal of literature for those who came after them. But they did encourage the converts to use the Amharic Bible.[30]

The lack of materials in different languages is one thing, but using Amharic, which is not the native language of the people, is another thing that adds to the

---

29. Fargher says that fifteen out of seventy-five believers in the class is not a success in the discipleship approach.

30. Fargher, *Origin*, 168.

complexity. In some Sunday meetings the speaker reads the Amharic Bible[31] which he understands just a little, then that has to be translated by another person who struggles to understand the speaker, and then the congregants have to bear with two confused people who have no idea what they are doing. One can imagine how such failures in communicating the gospel would negatively affect the lives of believers. There was a time in Wolaitta when believers were not allowed to raise goats because of their misunderstanding of the parable of goats and sheep in Matthew 25.

The protestant missionaries of the early days, like Peter Heyling (1607–1652), were not planning to create a new believing community but rather to revitalize and equip the existing Ethiopian Orthodox Church. They accepted the national church as a true church that needed more scriptural foundation and teaching in order to tackle all of the non-biblical traditions and myths that were incongruent with the gospel truth. It was only after their attempts failed that the missionaries turned to starting new churches. The SIM missionaries had a different philosophy from the very beginning. They were right in forming a separate community, because the strained relationship between the Ethiopian Orthodox Church and the southern people would have ruined their efforts. Their plan to form an alternative community that could influence the society was the correct decision.

According to Bosch, Luke's alternative community created by Jesus was a community of justice.[32] The poor, the gentiles, and the oppressed are invited to the kingdom of God. Girma Bekele writes, "What is clear is that Jesus and his movement were very appealing to the non-elite and lower-class communities who were seeking relief and escape from poverty, powerlessness and various forms of social and economic injustice."[33] Similarly, the new community formed in the south was inclusive and open to people from different lifestyles. For people who were abused and rejected, having a community that gave them a new identity and meaning in life meant a lot. The good news of the gospel and the new family unit it had created among different classes were attractive. The love and the respect of the believing community was infectious. The wider community observed how the believers offered practical help to each other in times of need. Some people joined the fellowship without really understanding

---

31. The Amharic version, which Fargher calls "a museum piece," is a wooden translation, which is difficult to understand even for native speakers let alone for people for whom Amharic is a second or a third language.

32. Bosch, *Transforming Mission*, 120.

33. Bekele, *In-Between People*, 212.

what they were getting into, because the warmth of the welcoming heart of the believers had a greater power to attract than all the punishment of the Italian colonizers and later the Marxist cadres. Discipleship requires a strong community that grows together in demonstrating the love of Christ and the kingdom of God on earth. As the community continues to reflect on its context and experience by the rereading of the Scripture, their mission is energized.

The Urban Pentecostal Stream

The third stream, the Pentecostal movement, began in the urban areas with educated young people and spilled over into the whole country. Pentecostals are the new arrivals in evangelical church history. Their roots go back to revival experiences in the 1950s and 1960s. Eshete, in his discussion about the source of the Pentecostal movement, rightly acknowledges the challenge of identifying a single root of Pentecostalism in Ethiopia. He writes, "Reconstructing the genesis of the Pentecostal movement in Ethiopia poses a considerable challenge to the historian, as it is difficult to provide an adequate explanation of the cause and manner of its emergence and of how it succeeded in sustaining itself as a movement."[34] In fact, any movement is a response to the existing context of the people.

The Social Context

Among the contextual issues of the fifties and sixties was the country's period of transition led by the modernization policy of the government. The urban youth were challenged by the transition and became involved in many kinds of philosophical parties and nationalistic movements. In the religious arena, the failure of the Ethiopian Orthodox Church to satisfy the spiritual hunger of the youth, the poorly contextualized nature of evangelical Christianity that lacked a connection with African traditional religion, and the lack of exuberance and prophetic utterance in the worship, all left the youth with many questions unanswered. The political turmoil, the social crisis, and the religious confusion left urban youth in disarray.

The external and internal shake up of things begged for change and answers. Many young people were attending English classes and revival meetings in Addis Ababa and the eastern towns of Harrar and Nazreth. The

---

34. Eshete, *Evangelical Movement*, 149.

Pentecostal experiences and the new energy added to the faith by underground meetings spread all over the place. The converts were so enthusiastic that some began to challenge the new Marxist ideology at its peak in the universities. Eshete writes, "The Pentecostal group daringly confronted those individuals who were promoting Marxism by taking time to study it so that they could confront the student radicals at intellectual and spiritual levels"[35] The student Marxist movement saw these few fanatics as a threat, and instigated persecution against them. The newly Pentecostal Christians were so passionate about their experience that they turned out to be aggressive evangelizers. The *Mulu Wongel* (Full Gospel) Church, the main indigenous fruit of the movement, was registered in 1967.

Because Pentecostal Christianity is more appealing to Ethiopian culture, with its focus on experience and demonstrations of power, the understanding of the conversion process shifted from instruction and ritual initiation to volitional dramatic experience that was expected to produce a dramatic transformation of life. In such event-oriented conversion, as Smith notes, conversion and salvation are confused.[36] Salvation is often understood as a one-time experience as one enters into the community of the saved group. Therefore, one is expected to remember the exact date and time of salvation so as to demarcate the entrance into the saved community. The emphasis on God's grace that is extended to sinners gives way to human volitional experience and unique encounter with the divine. The baptism of the Holy Spirit with its evidence of speaking in tongues replaces the step-by-step journey of the believer to spiritual maturity. Once people have the experience of the "second blessing" they are accepted as mature believers to be involved in the ministries of the church. Because of overemphasis on the spiritual gifts and experience, the initiation ritual of baptism loses its significance, unlike the situation in the missionary-planted churches.

It seems that the purpose of discipleship is to escort new believers in prayer until they reach the individual experience of the Holy Spirit. Once the new believers have such an experience they have the confidence to share about their experience with others and minister in different gifts. There exists a confusion regarding the role of conversion, water baptism, Spirit baptism and gifts of the Spirit. But it appears clear that the Spirit baptism becomes the foundation of conversion, and gifts of the Spirit authenticate the growth of the

---

35. Ibid., 67.
36. Smith, *Beginning Well.*

believer. Believers who have failed to speak in tongues and have no dramatic experience are considered immature or carnal Christians.

After the fall of the Derg in Ethiopia there were many revival meetings and conferences that focused on the filling of the Holy Spirit and special anointing. People prayed and fasted for a special touch from God, as if that were the ultimate goal of their lives. The emphasis of the mainline mission-planted churches on the intellectual process of discipleship was replaced by dramatic encounters that were considered to be real conversion and salvation experiences. The truth is that people do experience an encounter with God in prayer meetings and revival gatherings, but without a continuous discipleship process and renewing of their minds believers relapse to their old selves when they face challenges.

From the history and emphases of the Pentecostal movement we can deduce some contextualization and discipleship issues. It was a spontaneous movement out of the structure of the church, started by young people who were moved by their spiritual hunger. The movement spread under the persecution of the Marxist regime in the unstructured house churches. Here is how Eshete describes it:

> From the end of 1971 onward, the government increased its pressure on the secretly-operating Pentecostal cells while the latter were getting more defiant and insisted on their constitutionally granted rights of freedom of religious practice. The rising conflict culminated in the arrest of approximately 250 worshippers on Sunday, 27 August 1972. The legal and political aftermath of this incident did not turn out in favor of the Pentecostals, and they had to rely on secret meetings until the revolution of 1974.[37]

This movement was born in persecution and grew in it. Young lay people began the movement and everywhere they went they spread the news. Its urban origin gave the movement a handle to spread to small towns and villages. The members of the movement were bold to evangelize and share the gospel with others. They added passion to the intellectual Christianity introduced by the missionaries. However, their understanding of conversion as an event and experience, with the lack of discipleship materials to root converts in the Word of God, opened doors for much false teaching as the movement grew.

---

37. Eshete, *Evangelical Movement*, 68.

Conversion, Rituals and Community Formation in the Pentecostal Movement

The roots of Pentecostalism are to be found in the holiness movements in North America and other Western European countries, though there is no direct link to the Ethiopian movement. Pentecostalism emphasizes a new encounter with the Spirit of God and unique experience evidenced by speaking in tongues. Therefore, the emphasis is on a dramatic and sudden conversion experience to be witnessed publicly. The initial experience is so emphasized that people continue to speak about it years afterwards. Unlike the missionary-led Christianity that emphasized a cognitive conversion and verbal confession, the Pentecostal movement encourages an emotional and dramatic conversion, with the experience of the filling of the Holy Spirit. The conversion of the individual is only confirmed by the subsequent experience of the Spirit. Therefore, the continuous process of discipleship and structured confirmation classes was not closely followed as it was in the mission-planted churches. As a matter of fact, there were no trained ministers or pastors available to lead these new movements.

In many Pentecostal congregations, Spirit baptism overshadows water baptism. There is more preaching about "fresh anointing" than the remembrance of the death of Christ in communion. It is assumed that Spirit baptism rather than water baptism is what initiates one into the body of Christ. For instance, in the tradition of the Ethiopian Full Gospel Church, members who are not speaking in tongues or not "filled with the Spirit" are not eligible to be nominated for eldership, which shows that membership is through Spirit baptism.

The Pentecostal movement introduced more time for prayer and the demonstration of spiritual gifts, but at the expense of teaching time. They also gave more freedom for members to be involved in the worship service and to exercise their spiritual gifts, but these activities tended to squeeze out time for the word. However, people can easily fake some of these charismatic practices and appear to be changed without genuine transformation. Focusing on a single manifestation of conversion has made the movement ignore the other aspects of discipleship.

The Pentecostal movement from its early days attracted youth and diverse people groups. Because of its urban origin it is ethnically inclusive. Unlike the missionary-planted churches, which began their work among specific people groups and mainly in rural areas, the Pentecostal movement was a more urban, multiethnic movement. The community formation was unstructured, voluntary and spontaneous. The Pentecostal churches were often planted by lay people who started a prayer meeting which grew into a congregation when numbers increased.

The founders of the house prayer meetings became pastors and leaders as meeting groups turned into local churches. In such instances, members were shaped after their founders. Its unstructured beginning meant that there was no doctrinal consensus on various theological and administration issues, except for the main emphasis on Spirit baptism. The foundation of the community, therefore, was common experience rather than a common theological conviction.

The strength of the community thus depends on the individuals or the opinions of a few leaders rather than on an outlined faith statement. That makes the community vulnerable for conflict and division, and weakens the bonds between believers. In my observation, the mainline churches are struggling to transition from the mentality of structure to that of a movement, and the Pentecostal churches are finding it hard to become structured. On one hand, charismatic leadership without a discipleship structure becomes a one-man show. On the other hand, a rigid structure without a discipleship movement becomes a lifeless static tradition. The Pentecostal movement's contribution to the Ethiopian evangelical churches is in transforming Christianity into a passionate Spirit-filled movement that is not stifled by structures. Its weakness, though, is lack of an organized, Bible-based discipleship structure that is not just emotionally charged but also strong in doctrinal content and demonstrable practical application.

Analysis of the Evangelical Beginnings in Ethiopia

Though evangelical Christianity began in the northern part of Ethiopia, it actually flourished in the western, southern and urban Ethiopia because of the hard work of foreign and indigenous missionaries. It is the fruit of thousands who toiled in the harvest. Some lost their lives and others suffered persecution for the sake of spreading the gospel. No historian would play down the sacrifice made by those who willingly paid the price of following Christ in mission. When we discuss some of their shortcomings, it is not without acknowledging their hard work. I also acknowledge that any mission activity can only be properly analyzed and evaluated in its historical context. The following are some of the issues of contextualization and discipleship in the planting of the evangelical churches that contributed to today's crisis in discipleship.

Missed Opportunities

As described above, Christianity gave hope to the oppressed and hopeless people in the periphery. It was a precious opportunity for the missionaries and evangelists to properly disciple these converts – to root them in the Word of God. For several reasons, including lack of vernacular Scripture, materials and a holistic approach to discipleship, many converts struggled to live a transformed life. I can mention a few teaching moments that were missed in the discipleship process. First, the discipleship method was non-contextualized. It was conducted in a classroom setting, totally against the cultural setting of the believers. It was teaching biblical concepts without practical demonstration. The missionaries were not close enough to local believers to display the love of Christ. Certain days of instruction brought the converts and missionaries together but otherwise there were no opportunities for informal mentoring. The gated missionary stations kept the indigenous people away from their missionary mentors, creating a gap in the practical demonstration of Christian life.

Moreover, in the indigenous people's perspective the understanding of conversion was different from that of the missionaries. For the missionaries, conversion was a divorce from the cultural rituals and tradition, whereas for indigenous people it was not clear how to disconnect themselves from their culture. Fargher writes,

> They [the missionaries] viewed conversion as ideally an instant and total break with traditional religion. The expatriates themselves made no effort to be the core of a congregation but expected the converts to be naturally drawn to one another.[38]

The missionaries were not part of the new community; they guided from a distance. One can imagine that if the missionaries were not part of the local discipleship group, the chances of the converts misapplying the Scripture to their context would always be high. The relationship between the missionaries and the indigenous converts was not a close mentoring relationship. Leaders were not carefully discipled and instructed by the principles of the Scripture, so they were left to draw from their traditional worldview. "The KHC leaders were offended by instances of missionary paternalism and felt that the SIM was abandoning its work too quickly, and that it should have turned over

---

38. Fargher, *Origin*, 128.

its development projects to the church instead of to the government."[39] In a paternalistic relationship discipleship is unthinkable. The structure and procedures of the missionary organization played a part in straining the relationship between the missionaries and the indigenous leaders. In addition, administrative and cultural issues also disrupted the relationship, which ultimately affected the discipleship process.

Second, rituals were not properly contextualized to empower and encourage the converts in their discipleship journey. Rituals were misunderstood and not integrated into the Christian lives of the believers. Style of worship, for instance, is one of the areas that caused much disagreement among believers. Churches split and believers "church shop" for entertaining services. Worship ought to be directed to God; it brings believers to fellowship, and facilitates the discipleship journey. The missionaries, ignoring traditional cultural forms of worship, imported Western styles that created crises in different generations. Today many services lack a balanced approach towards worship. Not only worship but also other rituals, that would have communicated biblical concepts meaningfully in the oral culture, were ignored. For example, I mentioned above the use of monologue versus dialogue in the Hamar context.

Finally, the community of the early evangelical Christians, especially from the southern and western streams, struggled with identity issues. Alongside the power of the gospel, the general socio-political context that created an identity crisis made them receptive to the good news preached by the missionaries. However, because of all the cultural and ethnic values at work, the formation of a transformed kingdom community has not yet been accomplished successfully. Evangelicals were forced to stick together by the persecutions, instigated first by the Italian invaders and then by the Marxist regime, but now that the external pressure has gone, the unity of the evangelical church is crumbling in every direction. Community formation is based on ethnic and geographical location, and has failed to sustain the handling of diversity, so that in many parts of Ethiopia the church, rather than being a kingdom community, has turned out to be an ethnic affiliation.

---

39. Ethiopian historian Getachew Belete (*Elohe Ena Hale Luya*, 195) discusses those sentiments by the leaders of the KHC. It is a complicated relationship where cultural differences and undefined roles affected the relationship continually.

Persecution-Shaped Discipleship

After the Italian persecution, the evangelical churches had a brief break before the darkest Marxist persecution. At first the Marxists seemed to appeal to the people on the periphery. Believers thought the Marxist regime was God's agent to set the oppressed free. It was after some time, when the Marxist philosophy was disclosed, that many believers realized the danger, but some were beyond retreat, and gave up their faith. The Marxist persecution was a difficult time for people to come to Christ. Churches were closed and no public preaching of the gospel was allowed. Believers lived like they were under house arrest, with continual supervision by communist cadres. Those who wanted to come to Christ had to make a serious decision to suffer the consequences. Because of the Marxist government's harsh treatment and imprisonment of Christians, the conversion rate was not as high as at other times, but the church still grew. Many thought Christianity would soon be eradicated. However, people who were willing to die with Christ and counted the cost of discipleship joyfully joined the believing community. The believers shared their faith one-to-one and in-house fellowships. The love and care the believers had for one another was visible and enviable. Non-believers who were observing them wished to have such unity. Though publicly people rejected Christianity, they could not repudiate its influence and attraction. The way in which the believers handled the fierce persecution through strong community and discipleship reveals the grace of God and the potential of the church to defy hardship. I can identify four major effects of this persecution on the Christian community.

First, the persecution purified the church by sifting out the true believers from those who were merely nominal. Believers who were not committed enough to suffer for Christ left the church and joined the Communist party. Many believers, even pastors and evangelists, betrayed the church by revealing where they had hidden church resources. The genuine Christians maintained their faith and suffered for Christ. "For most evangelicals, the revolution drove Christianity into the heart of the people where faith was observed not by going to the church but by walking the talk."[40]

Second, the faithful believers bonded more strongly than ever as they faced the hardship. True unity and family spirit were evident among believers. Believers helped each other as they developed more passion for the return of Christ. No denominational affiliation, no ethic background, and no economic status separated the believers or hindered them from having fellowship. They

---

40. Eshete, *Evangelical Movement*, 302.

had one soul, one spirit and one purpose, which was to live and die for the name of Christ.

Third, in the small group fellowships and one-to-one meetings believers were able to mentor and disciple one another. The small group meetings were the only times when believers could pray and study the Bible together. New converts were divided between believers to be instructed. Converts were not rushed into ministry or leadership. They were given time to grow in their spiritual life.

Finally, believers developed a theology of suffering, which brought a deeper understanding of the cross of Christ. "Believers were seeking to attain to the closest possible imitation of Christ's passion and death. Love of Christ and hope of salvation through Christ alone was their inspiration and the essence of their faith. The martyr was a true disciple of Christ, one who follows the lamb wherever he goes."[41] The believers were focused on Christ and his second coming. Their aspiration was to emulate Christ in their lives and in their death.

At the downfall of the Marxist regime, when the ideology of communism with its secular worldview collapsed, there was a crisis in the society. The people who had trusted the secular Marxist philosophy and had followed it passionately were left in disarray when the regime changed. The communist ideology divided married couples, families and communities and made them fight with one another. It took some time for the society to heal after the fall of the regime. Thousands came broken-hearted to the church with repentance. The local churches were not prepared to deal with such great numbers of people and the discipleship system was not in place to mentor all the converts. The churches were overwhelmed by the sudden change of the context in their favor. The evangelical churches, being so excited with the opportunity to lead many to the kingdom of God, missed the key issue of discipleship in the maturing process. Rather than discipling converts in small groups, the churches adopted a celebratory approach through open-air meetings and conferences. The megachurch ideology was also introduced, which enabled people to hide in the crowd. As a result, the communist values and culture entered the church unfiltered, and were later manifested in the style of leadership.

After the collapse of the Marxist regime the church was the only stable organization that could offer secure relationship and healing. Trust in other social and political organizations had evaporated. Therefore, the church served as a refuge center for those who were going through psychological and social

41. Eide, *Revolution*, 226.

crises. This situation provided a motivation for conversion. As a matter of fact, many of those Marxist cadres, though they denied the existence of God publicly, were not really atheists; some called on the pastors to pray for them when they were sick. The collapse of the regime gave them the chance to practice what had been hidden in them and suppressed by the circumstances.

The key aspect to notice here is the lack of discipleship during the period of transition from persecution to freedom of worship. Dealing with the Marxist ideology that had been disseminated for seventeen years was not an easy task for the church. Many people were so involved in it that they needed a continual clean-up of those residual ideas and practices from the past. Renewing of their minds required intense training in the Word of God. On the other hand, the local churches were coming out of severe persecution where they had lost everything, and were recovering gradually. It was not an ideal time for the church to disciple so many people at once. The lack of strategic discipleship at this crucial juncture of the evangelical church led to many of the internal and external crises that the church faces today.

The Current Crisis in Ethiopian Evangelical Churches

It is an intriguing fact to learn from church history that churches handle suffering well yet fail to function well in a persecution-free context. The early apostolic church that spread like wildfire in the first few centuries lost its spiritual passion and zeal when Constantine converted to Christianity and the church was promoted to a lofty political status. Similarly, the Ethiopian evangelical churches seem to struggle to function in the current context of relative freedom of worship, in contrast to their time of persecution. Eshete writes,

> Freedom did not bring full blessing to the church, however. With freedom also came a reconfiguring of identity based on denominational lines. The challenge of a common threat had provided the anvil for unity that was indispensable. The newfound freedom, though not a major threat at this point, is not only testing the Evangelical Church but also presents a potential challenge unless due care is taken and if the lessons of the past are not well learned.[42]

---

42. Eshete, *Evangelical Movement*, 307.

Since the birth of the evangelical church in Ethiopia a century ago it has never experienced such a level of freedom of religion as it has enjoyed in the last two decades. There is freedom of worship and public appearance, despite the internal and systemic challenges the church is dealing with. The evangelical churches experienced persecution first by the Italian invaders for about five years, then under the brutal and anti-religion Marxist regime, and also rejection from the followers of traditional religion and adherents of the Ethiopian Orthodox Church. Many believers were imprisoned, flogged, and martyred for their faith. Many were treated as second-class citizens in their own country. The faithful stuck with Christ, but many backslid, joined the persecuting groups, and betrayed the church. With the fall of the Marxist regime things have changed. The church that had been persecuted severely during the Communist regime is now enjoying freedom at a level where even political meetings are opened with prayer. Many of those who persecuted the church rejoined the church after the collapse of the Communist regime. The house churches and underground fellowships came out bursting with people to rent new venues and the church multiplied in a few years.

However, the downside of all that is that the influence of the church in the community has significantly decreased and the ethical differences between Christians and non-Christians have become difficult to see. The persecution was external and physical, but now there is internal breakdown and spiritual complacency. G. Bekele captures this when he writes:

> With the establishment of the Federal Republic of Ethiopia the evangelicals are now enjoying unprecedented freedom. The question now is not whether or not the evangelicals are involved, but rather whether they are too involved, in a way that has allowed the intrusion of the current regime to jeopardize their prophetic integrity.[43]

It is a realistic fear that the evangelical churches in Ethiopia are in danger of losing their subversive and cutting edge prophetic voice. Many evangelicals are involved in different political parties, to the extent of recruiting church members for their respective parties. The believers' involvement was supposed to bring a positive influence on the community but the opposite is actually happening. Those who are deeply involved in politics do their best to make their voices heard and their ideas propagated in the church. In this process, as Bekele feared, the church is losing its prophetic integrity.

43. Bekele, *In-Between People*, 363.

The growth which the evangelical churches registered after the fall of the Derg Marxist regime was exponential. This growth does not reflect the churches' intentional mission strategy but rather the void in the socio-political environment created by the collapse of the Communist regime. This growth was not supported by strong discipleship. It is a numerical increase that has lacked spiritual depth. As a result, the evangelical churches have seen the rise of factions led by false teachers who focus on material and physical blessings at the expense of right doctrine and mission initiatives.

One of the areas in which one can observe the discipleship crisis in evangelical churches today is the lack of biblical and missional leadership in the local church and at the denominational level. The majority of current evangelical leaders and ministers are the fruit of the discipleship gap in the transition. Converts who learned all the language of the church and its systems and structure but were not transformed internally are assigned to lead the church. They are in the church with titles attached but they function according to either the cultural standards or the secular philosophy of leadership. A few genuine ministers suffer under such leadership and often end up with ongoing conflicts and church splits. Leaders lack vision and integrity to lead the church according to the will of God. Some come to their leadership position not on the basis of their spiritual gifts but on the basis of their ethnic connections and material possessions. The qualification for leadership becomes public performance rather than a demonstration of character.

Without discipleship in place it is unthinkable to expect godly leaders. Leaders are the fruit of discipleship, and lack of discipleship leads to leadership crises, which the evangelical churches are experiencing in Ethiopia. The leadership situation is so critical that some lose hope in the future of the church. Galgalo writes this with regard to churches in Africa:

> Some have come to the radical conclusion that the church in Africa has lost the gospel altogether and has built systems and institutions on ethnic bedrocks, and characteristically specialized in legalism, moralism and money matters – busy extorting members, with regards to the last point, if not extending the begging bowl to the West.[44]

There is a critical need to reform the churches in Africa regarding their focus, leadership and community formation. Christ-centered, discipleship-focused,

44. Galgalo, *African Christianity*, 2.

and community-based spirituality has to be restored in African churches to redeem the future.

To appropriately deal with the current challenges, the church in Ethiopia as well as the church global has to move its members from just membership to discipleship and from depending on certain individuals as missionaries to mobilizing the whole body of Christ for mission. To show how serious is the discipleship situation in the evangelical church in Ethiopia I will present some studies and reports regarding the contemporary context of the church. The main discussion points below are drawn from the survey done by the ECFE among its members, a survey among theological students regarding the health of the church, and a leadership workshop that analyzed the current status of the churches.

ECFE Mission Survey Results

From May 2004 to May 2005 the Evangelical Churches Fellowship of Ethiopia, in partnership with Dawn Ministries, conducted research that they later published under the title *National Mission Research*. The project was led by Lemma Degefa, a prominent contributor in the area of church leadership. There were some indications in the research that the evangelical churches started to see some of the seeds of the current crisis back then, a decade ago. However, being part of an oral culture, the leaders of the evangelical churches have not paid attention to the published warnings of the researchers. If the leaders had responded to the issues mentioned, we would have a different story. The research was not as comprehensive as one would wish, but it accurately reflected the state of the evangelical churches in Ethiopia. It was the first of its kind; the church needs more of such research to listen to the culture and to read the signs of the times. The ECFE should be applauded for this venture, but also criticized for not continuing such studies. This is neither the place nor the time to discuss the research in detail, but I would like to mention some of the findings that are descriptive of the situation of the churches in Ethiopia.

First, the findings show that churches have an ineffective approach to discipleship, and that the evangelical church leaders are not satisfied with it.

> Almost all local church leaders have shared their concern that the ministry of discipleship is ineffective. Among the other things lack of trained disciple makers in the church, lack of well-

developed and contextualized teaching material and poor teaching methodology are the major causes of shallow discipleship.[45]

A decade ago it was a concern; today it is a real problem that affects the mission of the church. From the above description of the church one can deduce three key needs in the church. (1) There is a lack of disciples and disciple makers. Of course this should be a real concern for the church. But it also makes one ask, what is the duty of the church leadership if they are not making disciples? If the church leadership is concerned about the discipleship situation, why should they not do something about it? The leadership is supposed to devise solutions for such critical problems. (2) As the research indicates, the materials for proper discipleship are lacking. Since the fall of the Marxist regime, Bible schools at all levels, seminaries and graduate schools have been opened, but the education system is not discipleship-based and the issues are not discussed in a contextual way. Practical and relevant materials to address the needs of believers are not available for pastors and leaders to work with. This shows the need for theological schools to take leadership in the area of discipleship training. (3) The appropriate discipleship methodology is not yet introduced. The classroom instruction-based discipleship is not producing disciples mature enough to face the reality of life in the community. Churches have disorganized discipleship programs that are not contextualized and not strategic.

Second, the budget allocation of churches reveals that their priority is not mission or church planting. One of the survey questions focuses on the yearly spending budget of the churches. According to the study, 59.2 percent of the evangelical churches have no budget allocated for church planting. Moreover, "out of the 40.8% churches who allocate budget for church planting, only 3% allocate more than 60% of their annual budget for church planting."[46] Where is the money going? What else is being done in the churches? After the reestablishment of religious freedom, the evangelical churches were under pressure both from the government and from the believers to have a piece of land and to put a building on it. During this study, 60 percent of the evangelical churches were using rented venues for the Sunday worship meetings; after a decade there may be a few changes but the need for buildings is still huge. Therefore, the resources in many evangelical churches have been directed to church buildings, securing a piece of land and other materials that

---

45. Degefa, *ECFE*, 57.
46. Ibid., 54.

are required for Sunday services. The focus of the churches has shifted into securing buildings rather than sending missionaries and planting churches. Discipleship is shelved for now because of these other priorities.

Third, the current growth of the church is slower. There are not as many converts, but more people are moving from church to church. The findings show that the evangelical churches are not keeping pace with the population growth of the country in general. The number of evangelicals was 1.1 million in 1968 and in 2005 it was reported to be about ten million – maybe a little over. Today it is estimated at about twenty million evangelical believers in Ethiopia, where the population is approaching one hundred million. There is an increase in number among evangelicals, but evangelicals are still the minority and the rate of growth has started to slow down. There are still unreached people groups in the border areas and many churches are reluctant to get involved in cross-cultural mission. There is very little research being done regarding strategic plans to spread the gospel to the unreached people groups. Rather, the tendency in the urban areas is to build megachurches at the expense of the small churches. The focus is shifting from building the kingdom of God to building a kingdom of famous individuals.

Fourth, the research shows that leadership crises and church conflicts are increasing alarmingly.[47] These include conflicts between denominations and conflicts within the denominations and local churches. Church leaders are out in public courts arguing about material things and benefits. In many places, whenever there is an election in the local church there is tension among believers – members are divided along ethnic and geographical lines. Bekele describes this disturbing situation:

> During the pre-FDRE governments, evangelicals had made constant appeals to local officials, and even to the Emperor, for protection against the radical EOTC opposition; now, by contrast, it has become customary for contemporary evangelical churches to seek FDRE's intervention to separate them from each other, as they are unable to resolve internal conflicts.[48]

The evangelical churches fought the Marxist regime strongly through their unity and cooperation. When one church was closed the other churches were willing to host the members. House fellowships were not organized along denominational lines, but believers in the same neighborhood invited each

---

47. Ibid., 58.
48. Bekele, *In-Between People*, 364.

other in love. Currently, however, it is difficult enough for a single denomination to worship and serve God in peace and unity, let alone different denominations meeting together in one place. The leadership of the church must share the main blame for all these conflicts and divisions because they are either caused by them or by people who are influenced by them.

Theological Students' Evaluation of the Church

In my teaching career at the Ethiopian Graduate School of Theology I always encouraged my students to stay connected with the church during their studies. In my Church and Mission course every year I have asked my students to do a short survey of their local congregations. The students are from different denominational backgrounds – evangelical, Pentecostal, contemporary, and mainline – and their involvement in the church varies from being a member to being in leadership as a pastor, worship leader and the like. The content of the survey focuses on the vision, mission, passion, focus, vibrancy and community influence of the church. The results of these surveys over three consecutive years show that 2 percent of students think their churches are healthy, 25 percent of the students think their church is growing towards becoming a healthy church, 44 percent of the students believe that their churches are spiritually sick, 27 percent of the students think their churches are *seriously* sick spiritually, and 2 percent of the students think their churches are spiritually dead. Of course, one cannot come to a strong conclusion on the basis of such a mini-survey, but it gives an indication that people including leaders are not satisfied with where the church is heading. Almost 73 percent of the students felt their churches were not healthy in terms of vision, mission, passion and influence. Mission springs from the identity of the church and the church has to be healthy to create a kingdom community.

Warning Signs

The discipleship issue is also a concern of church leaders and pastors. A few years ago, the short-lived but influential Amharic magazine *Mathetes* was published with the headline, "The Church in Ethiopia Is in Danger!"[49] The magazine discussed the contemporary evangelical context of Ethiopian churches based on interviews with prominent Ethiopian ministers including

---

49. Mengiste Ab, "The Church in Ethiopia Is in Danger!"

Dr Fanta, Ato Bulicha and others. The basic thrust of the articles was a warning to the churches that the direction in which the church is heading is not biblical and not in accordance with God's will. The spread of "health and wealth" gospel preachers and self-promoted prophets, resulting in confused believers, is not a sign of a healthy church. The fragmentation of the churches, with lack of accountability, has left people to do what they feel like doing. This magazine warned leaders and members that tough times of spiritual crisis are ahead. The issue is subtle because to an observer the church appears to be growing and increasing, but deep inside the foundation is shaking. As well as these written articles and the ministers' warnings, the practical lives of believers among the non-believers demonstrate the lack of discipleship among Christians. It seems that evangelical believers have lost their grip on biblical foundations and are being carried along by the culture and contemporary trends.

The Leaders Respond

Leaders, ministers and theological educators have observed the problem and have not ignored it altogether. Individuals, institutions and churches have done what they can. Presentations, workshops and studies have been done at various levels, though these have not been comprehensive in nature.

April 2015 was a promising month for evangelical churches in Ethiopia. Concerned groups and ministries put together a workshop for church leaders on the current spiritual context of evangelical churches in Ethiopia. About five hundred leaders gathered to listen to the presentations focused on three main areas, namely, quality of spiritual life, quality of leadership, and quality of scriptural teaching and doctrine. The participants listened attentively and prayed with tears, asking for forgiveness for not doing enough to intervene in the situation. The presentations can be summarized as follows: The church in Ethiopia is experiencing a spiritual life crisis that is manifested in declining spiritual vitality, distorted biblical teaching and lack of servant leadership; therefore, the evangelical churches have to identify the problems, repent of their negligence, and go forward with new commitment to discipleship and renewal of the church. The church leaders agreed on the issues mentioned and at the end of the workshop the recurring question from the participants was, what has to be done at what level to deal effectively with this spiritual crisis. The papers of the workshop are compiled as a book, but beyond being a warning signal for the churches and ministers there has not been a strategic response to the issues raised.

The reality is that the evangelical churches in Ethiopia, though they might appear externally to be growing, are experiencing deep crisis internally. Churches are full of people, revival meetings are held in many stadiums, and new churches are being opened every week, it seems. But the strong positive influence of the church on the wider community, that once existed even during the Marxist regime, is now fading away. Evangelical churches are rather influenced by the political reality of the time and they struggle to deal with racial and economic issues that have divided the church with bitter conflict. The unity in Christ that has been promoted for years and the diversity that has been celebrated as a blessing is now overwhelmed by ethnocentrism and egocentrism.

Bekele provides this quotation about the contemporary church in Ethiopia from an interview with Ato Shifera, the former president of the Ethiopian Kale Heywet Church:

> . . . seemingly there is explosive growth, but it is obesity; there is colorfulness, but in many senses it is external; there is visible affection, but it is superficial, not from the heart; supposedly, there is submissiveness, but as long as one's view is accepted; there is tolerance, but only temporary; there is worship, but with no sign of the fear of God; there is religiosity, but it is not substantiated with testimony.[50]

The observation of this leader indicates that some things we see evidently are not genuine; rather, it is a show disconnected from life. Such double life is a result of poor discipleship or the lack of it altogether.

From my personal observations, readings, and discussions with church leaders, the current context of the church in Ethiopia can be summarized in three areas: power, passion, and purpose.

First, the church without power. The evangelical churches of Ethiopia were born in a hostile environment and grew through persecution. In the late nineteenth and early twentieth centuries the religio-political context was not open for the ministry of missionaries and for the planting of new churches. Missionaries were not welcomed either by political leaders or by the Ethiopian Orthodox Church priests. Yet the small beginning in several places spread and the evangelical churches today claim about 20 percent of the general population. The evangelical church that was born in a difficult environment continued to face persecution in its infancy. Though imprisoned

---

50. Bekele, *In-Between People*, 366–367.

and rejected publicly, the believers made many disciples in private homes and group gatherings. The believers, though persecuted, attracted many to join the small group meetings. Though numerically in the minority, their influence was beyond their numbers. They had a powerful witness that could not be neglected by the persecuting world.

The current evangelical churches in Ethiopia are losing their power of influence in word and deeds. The strong Scripture-based spiritual life is replaced by all sorts of emotional experiences. The life quality of leaders is not shining out in the community. Christian professionals are losing the salty presence among their coworkers. The evangelical churches that are expected to lead the society and work towards the coming of the kingdom of God are yoked unequally with the current system. The church has not only lost its power to influence but also its power to attract others to its fellowship. Because of the continual conflict and tension in the evangelical churches, people from other religions hear and harden their hearts from time to time. In those difficult days of the persecution the evangelical community was so connected with each other that they attracted many people to their fellowship. When religious freedom came, the evangelical churches grew in number but lost the depth of love for one another. For the church of Christ, losing its influence and leadership position in the community is a serious thing.

Second, passion for material things has replaced passion for God. Believers who longed for the presence and power of the Lord have cooled off, chasing the temporary satisfaction of material things. In the persecution years the believers put their hope in Christ, who is the only source of their strength, now their hopes are more about moving to the West and enjoying an easy life, than about moving to heaven to be with the Lord. Passion for God has been lost in the search for ethnic and national identity. The worship songs, the prayers and the preaching are more directed to material blessings than longing for the kingdom of God in the midst of his people. "Your kingdom come, your will be done" is changed to "My blessing come as I do my will." Those who were under persecution worshipped the Lord in prison cells with great joy. They were passionate about their life in Christ, but today's evangelical believers fail to worship in Spirit and in truth even though all the musical instruments are organized. Believers have lost passion for Christ as they search for teachers who will scratch their itching ears.

The evangelical churches have lost not only passion for God but also passion for lost souls. In the days when talk about Christ was banned, believers dared to proclaim his lordship, but today, when there are so many opportunities, the fact that so many believers are not active in witnessing is mind-boggling. Churches trust evangelistic crusades and healing meetings rather than one-to-one evangelism. Evangelism has been left to full-time ministers, while believers are more concerned about their own personal prophesies and desires.

Third, consider the purpose of the church. The church is the called people of God, as the Bible declares – called for a purpose, and called for work. The church's loss of its main purpose puts it on the same level as any other gathering of people. Missing the core purpose of the church has led to all kinds of strife and division. Individually, believers are part of the body of Christ; corporately, they are unified by the blood of Jesus and the task given to them by the Lord. Each Christian is gifted to serve the body of Christ, not to elevate themselves and gather followers, but Ethiopian evangelicals are more into celebrity-type leaders than servants in the fellowship of the body of Christ. The church is struggling to deal with ethnic divides, to handle language issues, and to appoint godly leaders for the churches. The unity that came through the finished work of Christ is undermined and replaced by new ethnic and geographical connections that damage the image of the church. I could say much more about the challenges facing the church. My purpose is not to paint a hopeless picture of the church but to promote awareness of the reality. The church belongs to God. However messy it gets, Christ the head can clean it up. We are called to work with him.

So far, the context of the Ethiopian evangelical churches and the need for contextual discipleship has been explained. Now let us turn to what discipleship really is and how it will be done.

6

Strategies for Effective Contextualized Discipleship

The issue of discipleship is an ecclesiological issue, an academic issue and a leadership issue. It concerns everyone in the body of Christ. Without discipleship we can only expect either the spiritual death of the church or the physical death of members in racial or ethnic violence, as happened in Rwanda. Christianity without discipleship fails to influence the world, fails to help its members mature, and fails to advance the kingdom of God. This is a crucial time for the church worldwide to go back to the basics of being and making disciples. The future of the church depends not on its multi-million building complexes, attractive worship bands or popular preachers, but on true disciples who declare Christ in their lives and testimonies. The global church must prioritize discipleship, thinking strategically and integrating it into all the ministries of the church.

A discipleship strategy has to be designed in a biblically sound and contextually effective way. Though we can learn from the diverse experience of believers, we should draw from Scripture the basic principles of our contextual strategies. Because of the nature of discipleship, every element must be adapted according to the socio-religious context of the believers. For example, in places where believers are persecuted, the design would be different than in other places. According to James Samra, the contemporary church can draw at least two principles from Paul's strategy of discipleship in the early church. First, Paul treated believers whom he discipled as equals in the body of Christ. Though he was an apostle and a church planter, he respected and trusted his disciples as brothers and sisters in Christ.

> For example, he referred to Timothy and Silvanus as apostles with him, even though they were clearly subordinate to him in both

authority and Christian maturity. He called Apollos a coworker (1 Cor 3:5–9) and Timothy a fellow-worker (1 Thess 3:2) and a brother (2 Cor 1:1; Col 1:1), even though Timothy was his son in the faith (1 Tim 1:2; 2 Tim 1:2).[1]

Effective discipleship begins with a positive attitude towards the people whom God has entrusted to us, regardless of their spiritual status. People's lives should be taken seriously and our investment should be wholehearted.

Second, Paul was willing to invite people to imitate him. He was not pointing to himself as the ultimate model, but people could see Christ demonstrated through him. As he lived a life that was committed to Christ he modeled the way and he had the confidence that he could be emulated by his followers. Spiritual leadership is about following Christ and helping others to follow him. It is not about power or position but it is about imitating Christ. Paul, who was busy proclaiming the gospel, teaching and encouraging believers everywhere, spared time to mentor a few leaders whom he selected to continue the ministry when he was gone. As leaders, serving structures and procedures without demonstrating Christ in our lives is incongruent with biblical teaching.

For individual apostles like Paul and for the communities of believers in the early church, the primary agenda of their ministry was disciple making. It is through that emphasis that the churches grew exponentially despite all the persecution they went through.

> At the end of the second century, Tertullian (c. AD 160–220) would boast to the Roman authorities in Carthage: "We are but of yesterday, and we have filled every place among you – cities, islands, fortresses, towns, marketplaces, the very camp, tribes, companies, palace, senate, forum – we have left nothing to you but the temple of your gods."[2]

Tertullian's claim of taking over the territories of the known world of the day in spreading the good news of Christ can only be imagined in a context of strong Christian community.

In the early church the focus of individual leaders was on investing in people and creating a natural connection between the lives of believers and their mission. Paul Hartog, in his article "Learning from Patristic Evangelism and Discipleship" points out that there was an organic relationship between

---

1. Samra, "Biblical View," 229–230.
2. Hartog, *Contemporary Church*, 29.

evangelism and discipleship in the early church. That organic relationship made the church strong and its witness authentic. First, the witness of the early church was socially integrated. Believers, though persecuted, did not withdraw from their social context but lived faithfully as both citizens of their respective countries and heavenly citizens. There were no conferences or open-air meetings, but every believer was an evangelist among the people where God had placed him or her. The preaching of the gospel was not assigned to a certain few full-time apostles, but the entire community was responsible to live Christ-centered lives and to witness about him voluntarily. Once the converts had made the decision to become believers, the community focused on discipleship. Rituals were administered meaningfully to strengthen their commitment and to remind the believers of their purpose in life.

> The rich imagery attempted to communicate through symbolism the work of Christ in believers both in their initiation and in their continued communion in the church. The symbolic action served an educational function in congregations where the members were largely illiterate.[3]

The formation of the community began with the transformation of their imagination that was shaped by Christ. In addition, the contextual approach to discipleship training created an understanding that was deep and transformative.

There are three lessons we can learn from the early church that can help in our attempts to make disciples. First, the mission of the church has to be focused on making disciples. If the mission of the church is divorced from the maturing of believers through discipleship the church faces an uphill battle to effectively accomplish its task. Our evangelism must incorporate a discipleship system where believers do not just begin their spiritual journey but also continue into a committed life. Second, the discipleship process has to incorporate rituals and symbols to deepen the understanding of the believers in practical terms. Rituals enhance and intensify the believers' journey as they face various challenges in their faith. Finally, as the early church was intentional in community formation, the contemporary church must organize communities of disciples. Their communities were from diverse socio-economic backgrounds but unified under one purpose. No racial or ethnic background became an obstacle for community formation.

---

3. Ibid., 50.

Based on these lessons we have drawn from the early church and the need for a contextual strategy for discipleship, three key issues must be taken into consideration in our contemporary context. These are: contextual education and training of believers, appropriate church structure to facilitate discipleship, and the establishment of discipleship as a tradition or culture of the church. If we address the need for transformative education, appropriate structure and established discipleship culture, the church can effectively begin to accomplish its mission. Discipleship begins with the decision of an individual or community to follow Christ, and that has to be followed by training the disciples and placing them in the body of Christ structured as a community that continues to practice and develop a culture of discipleship.

Christian Education for Discipleship

Discipleship involves teaching. Converts have to be taught in ways they can understand in order to make decisions. Contextually appropriate communication and a suitable curriculum gives a strong foundation to the discipleship process. Christian education is at the heart of any discipleship process. Without an effective teaching and training system it is difficult to turn believers into disciples. That is why the apostolic church began their discipling process with strong biblical teaching. "They devoted themselves to the apostles' teaching and to fellowship, to the breaking of bread and to prayer. Everyone was filled with awe at the many wonders and signs performed by the apostles" (Acts 2:42–43). It is through that devoted teaching of the apostles that the foundation of Christianity was built.

As the center of Christianity shifts to the non-Western world, one of the expectations is that the church in the non-West could take some leadership in theological areas. The practical and experience-based African Christianity has to add academic depth as well as discipleship strength. Lack of strong contextual theological education has been the struggle of non-Western churches and has contributed to the challenges the church is facing today. Western curricula introduced to the non-Western context have failed to address the needs of believers in terms of discipleship. Believers have been obliged to study issues that have nothing to do with their day-to-day lives. As a result, cultural values continue to dictate the believers' behavior, even at the expense of scriptural teachings. That is not to undermine the contribution of the non-Western world to global Christianity. For instance, African Christianity has passion, zeal and exuberance that can be shared with the global church, but zeal without knowledge and understanding can lead one in a wrong direction. Andrew Walls rightly noted this reality:

> That Africa will bring gifts to the church is widely recognized, and many see those gifts as including zeal for Christ, unembarrassed witness to him, energy and delight in worship, and fervency in prayer, all of which will bless the wider church. But Africa must bring other gifts too. Intellectual and theological leadership of the Church must increasingly come from Africa, Asia and Latin America . . . There must be excellence, world-quality capacity for leadership. Africa, together with Asia and Latin America, will increasingly have to be the power house of Christian thought.[4]

Theological reflection and practical experience should be integrated and balanced to be credible and trustworthy in the global scene. In Africa the above-mentioned qualities of the church lack deep reflection on Scripture. African believers earnestly pray and passionately witness to others, but at times those practices are ill motivated, and neither glorify God nor benefit the church. For example, Africans have a communal culture, and it is natural for one to be in a group, but sometimes those groups are founded along racial and ethnic lines, and that goes against the biblical value of oneness in Christ. Theological education has to deal with such contextual issues in order to transform those ethnic biases and inclinations. Therefore, theological leadership requires in-depth understanding of our own context in the light of Scripture in order to share the principles with the wider body of Christ. To come to such a level, the role of transformative Christian education is crucial.

The existing discipleship training in many churches comprises knowledge-based and information-focused teaching that does not take the whole of life into consideration. Believers are often evaluated by their classroom attendance and involvement in activities of the church rather than in their real-life situations. Theological schools promote academic excellence at the expense of character development. The educators are expected to impart knowledge not life. Theology students are encouraged to entertain theological concepts from the Western context and model theologians from the West. For some, reading liberal theologians from the West confuses their understanding rather than creating clarity. As a result, they disconnect themselves from the contextual reality of their people as they keep dialoguing with theologians from a different context. As a matter of fact, theological educators, in addition to passing on

---

4. Walls, "The Significance of Global Christianity," 6.

information, have a key role to play in making disciples. It is through formal and informal discipling that lives are shaped – not just through lectures. For example, during the Marxist regime where all the churches were closed and no formal theological education existed in Ethiopia, the believers trained new converts by modeling the Christian life and giving instruction in their private homes. The churches grew and the believers were strong in their commitment to Christ.

If Christian education is to contribute to disciple making in the church, the educational philosophy implemented in the churches is of monumental importance. The education culture has to be revisited to address the contemporary issues of the church. Tim McDonough in his approach to educational philosophy advocates initiation over indoctrination as the more effective education strategy. According to McDonough, indoctrination is the fulfillment of educational requirements without supporting it with rational and practical truth. Initiation, on the other hand, is a process of enabling and empowering through an integrated approach. He writes, "Initiation is a pedagogy which, properly understood, teaches students to engage in the differentiation, articulation, and transformation of constitutive elements of culture."[5] Cultural initiation lifts the person up to a different social level and integrates him or her into the community with different dynamics. Theological education should help students to discern and make right judgments, to explain their position in the body of Christ, and to become mature to a level at which they become agents of transformation. Because the spiritual journey is continuous, ongoing education should accompany believers so that they understand faith in different stages of their journey.

Theological education that follows the indoctrination model dichotomizes life inside the classroom and outside of it. Many theological educators are not disciples of Christ though they are expected to teach theology and prepare students for ministry; this defeats the purpose of theological education. Theological education divorced from disciple making fails to serve the church and its purpose. Our purpose in Christian education should be both producing excellent academicians and faithful Christ-like disciples who transform their social contexts through positive influence. If the places where ministers are trained de-emphasize discipleship, then it is no wonder that churches fail to make disciples. Producing theologians after the heart of the world's scholars is

5. McDonough, "Initiation," 711.

one thing, but theologians after God's heart is what is needed in the kingdom of God.

> Initiation is a pedagogy meant to help students work creatively and progressively within a particular normative and symbolically constructed field, especially in response to both internal and external challenges. It is a pedagogical means to both transmit knowledge of a tradition by teaching students to master a symbolic code and repertoire, and also to engage them in the development of their own capacities to manipulate that code to create alternative pronouncements and judgments in the face of historical and normative challenges to the system.[6]

It is through this enablement that education prepares a believer to understand the message of the gospel, to live it and to share it with others. Key to this initiation approach is preparing the student to be creative in response to the contextual issues, and, on the basis of the knowledge gained through instruction, to construct strategies to deal with challenges among the believers. For instance, one of the challenges among the African Christian communities is ministering to demon-possessed people. Rather than just teaching a theory about the power of God it would be better to assign the students to different congregations to minister to the people who are under the bondage of demonic influence. Through such an approach the believing communities learn to disciple one another as they reflect on the Scripture in their own social context. Institutions should tune their approach and adopt ways that can equip students to disciple others. Seminaries establish the relationship between action and reflection by facilitating reflection on the praxis of God and the ongoing mission of the church in the world. In this reflection the fulfillment of the individual's present calling is paramount, while the loss of self in service to others leads to spiritual maturity. The relationship between theory and practice is complex and dynamic within the missional model. Institutions should promote a theology that is reflective, based on calling, and balanced in theory and practice. The mission of the church must be practiced through continuous dialogue between action and reflection.

Different cultural contexts have different educational needs that should be taken into consideration. Though the fundamental principles of Christian education are similar, every context requires contextually appropriate methods to effectively communicate the message. For example, an African

---

6. Ibid., 721.

Christian education system has to take into consideration at least the following four issues: orality, practicality, power encounters and community-based instruction. First, African culture is an oral culture that prefers face-to-face instruction. Communication is mainly through oral communication and storytelling. People in the villages train their children through modeling and telling stories. When Christianity was introduced to Africa a new education method was introduced with it: formal education that often fails to address the issues on the ground. Education curricula in the church copied the model that was rooted in Western Enlightenment; it improved the intellectual capacity of believers but failed to transform lives. The renewal of hearts and minds takes place in a culturally contextualized education system that challenges believers to see their context critically through the lenses of the Scripture. In communal cultures, events, festivals and celebrations are good moments for intentional discipleship. Adults learn through practical involvement in which a mentor works with the gifts and talents of the believers in his or her group.

Second, African culture emphasizes practical action; it looks for relevant contemporary issues that can be applied immediately. Because of the socio-political challenges of the continent, there is a great need for immediate healing and encouragement. This is probably why many prosperity preachers get a good hearing in Africa. They promise immediate relief and deliverance from spiritual and physical suffering. On the contrary, many theologians focus on the future kingdom of God and point believers to the millennium that will come when Christ returns. Though it is a biblical perspective, it is one-sided, and ignores the immediate situation of the individual. Discussion about the future has to begin with the current need. Otherwise, for many it is a philosophical game of theories that have no practical value. In the words of Miller, "Theory that is not practical is empty, and practice without theory is blind. Systematic and historical theology belongs to practical theology; when divorced from one another, emptiness and blindness result."[7] The need for a balanced approach in Christian education cannot be overemphasized.

Third, African culture deals with evil spirit powers as a serious problem. Theological reflection that ignores spiritual encounters in the African context fails to speak to a core issue. Theologians with impressive ideas but lacking supernatural power to set people free from the spiritual bondage of the devil are ignoring a crucial issue in African spirituality. As S. Muriti rightly observes, "Pastors trained in many African theological institutions are ill equipped to

---

7. Miller, "Religious Education," 418.

deal with this issue. Teachings in African theological schools that faithfully follow the missionary curriculum have failed to respond adequately to the person afflicted by spiritual powers."[8] The earlier Western theologians thought of spiritual warfare as a superstitious primal religious practice, though they read it all over the Scripture. In African culture, spiritual power is always an issue and is the concern of believers and non-believers alike. Therefore, demonstration of God's power gets more attention than eloquent preaching or convincing philosophical theories. A contextual theological education equips the student to demonstrate both knowledge and spiritual power.

Fourth, we have to realize that in African culture education is community based. It does not elevate individual achievement or excellence, rather it is wisdom owned and shared by the community. In my own grade school we shared exam answers, though it was wrong, because we wanted no one to fail. What mattered for me was that all of us should get a passing grade, rather than one of us exhibiting an extraordinary talent. In many theological seminaries students learn to compete rather than to cooperate. This does not sit comfortably with African culture. They make every effort to become the first person in their classes, and unfortunately they take this attitude with them to their field of ministry, and continue to compete with their fellow leaders.

In conclusion, the role of Christian education in making disciples in the local church is foundational. Christian educators should become disciple makers and share their lives as well as their knowledge. Below I will refer to some perspectives on theological education that would be helpful in devising strategies for training in disciple making; modifications would have to be made for different cultural contexts. First, Latin American educationalist E. Fernandez outlines seven key points for effective theological education, and I would like to mention five:[9]

1. Knowledge is constructed not transmitted. An educator should disciple a student to construct a practical and theoretical knowledge that is relevant to his/her context.

2. Avoid blind adoption of programs and curricula. Curriculum should be contextually developed to appropriately deal with the issues of the context.

---

8. Muriti, "Contextual Theological Education," 49.
9. Fernandez, "Engaging Contextual Realities."

3.   Design to shape new mental models of reality as well as new ways of interacting with the reality. Helping students to have an imaginative skill that addresses the needs of the context is crucial.

4.   Effective Christian educators do not merely transfer information but help students to build a Christian worldview.

5.   To be effective educators we have to keep in continuous dialogue with the changing nature of the world and its implications including one's own ministry.

Fernandez's five points advocate contextualized education for the transformation of individual students and their wider context in transforming worldviews that dictate the entire culture.

N. Rooms also proposes seven theses for transformative theological education. Such education, he says, has to be:[10]

1.   reflective in balancing theory and practice;

2.   contextual, that is, relevant to the context;

3.   imaginative, which involves both heart and mind;

4.   spiritual, which is done with prayer;

5.   "glocal" in focus – both global and local;

6.   relational – it bonds the teacher and student;

7.   and a service to the body of Christ. Theology that serves the church benefits the church.

If theological education is to serve the church's call to practice discipleship, it has to incorporate different dimensions of training. From the educational philosophies of Fernandez and Rooms we can summarize at least four principles: discipleship-based theological education has to be contextual, spiritual, reflective and transformative. It has to be contextual because it must speak to the context; it has to be spiritual since God is Spirit and those who study him must serve him in spirit; and Christian education has to be reflective and transformative so that thoughts and actions work together to bring holistic changes to the entire world.

---

10. Rooms, "Theological Education."

Church Structure for Discipleship

The church is more fragmented than ever. Church conflicts and splits are observed everywhere. Believers are less committed to their denominational traditions. This is the post-denominational era. Church shopping and switching from denomination to denomination is rising. Church fights over positions and material things expose the weakness of the church before the world. Where there is fragmentation there is no strong discipleship. In this lack of unity the church loses its foundation for authentic discipleship. In growing Ethiopian congregations, believers fight over what language to use in the worship; on occasion, chaotic clashes have been stopped only by police intervention. Unity is an area that has been drastically affected by the secular culture of the contemporary world. Though church members may be assembling in one building, their hearts are divided. Believers are feeling more independent and individualistic than ever, and church leaders have had to devote significant time to making peace among the churches and believers in different congregations. This is the biggest obstacle for discipleship.

One of the reasons for this fragmentation is that the church is not organized according to the scriptural vision of organic unity. The church is not discipleship-oriented at its foundation. Often the structure of the church is copied from the culture or the secular political world. In the New Testament we see glimpses of church structures that were created for organizing God's people for God's mission. The structures served to facilitate the actual involvement of believers in mission as they discipled converts. That is probably why the New Testament has not given us a blueprint for church structure, but only flexible strategies for charismatic team leadership. According to Smith, the church in Ephesus, under the pastoral ministry of Timothy, appears to have been more structured than the church in Thessalonica. Smith writes,

> The New Testament structured and shaped the identities of the people of God while using cultural expressions to help them live faithfully under Christ's lordship. Within these cultural expressions of organizing and living from the first century, we see a vast array of communities focused on the return of Christ.[11]

Smith points out three structures observable in the New Testament, all based on the Greco-Roman cultural context, namely, the household, voluntary associations and philosophical schools. These three cultural models of

---

11. Smith, "Missional Communities," 197.

community formation and social structure were used by Paul and other apostles to structure spiritual groups. These are not traditional church structures but existing cultural settings that believers used to organize themselves in every city and village. These were structures for evangelism and discipleship. The church structures were there to feed the discipleship structures already established in the community. The church met on Sundays for celebration but the discipling activity was continuous in the community on the week days.

In the current church situation, structures and forms not only create a blockage between the people of God and their mission, but they also tend to serve individual interests rather than the kingdom of God. The structures serve only the believing community and are confined within church offices and positions. Some church structures are copied from different contexts and fail to function in a new context. The mission of the church is often stranded on account of structural complications. Some decisions take years and years because of the line of commands, while those on the field waiting for those decisions continue to face many difficulties. The structure of the church needs to be a discipleship structure that promotes and facilitates the growth of the congregation. At every level of the community, creating a chain of discipleship structures helps members to be accountable to each other in their spiritual journey.

Leaders should serve people by using the structures, not abuse people to preserve the structures. Leaders are servants of God's people assigned to work at building up the body of Christ according to their gifting and talents. Wise leaders use the structures to make disciples. Using the privilege given to them by the structure, they can influence people to grow in their spiritual lives. It is through a living connection and relationship that the church not only serves its own body but also the world at large. The challenge in the global church today is to find a balance between a stiff and rigid structure and a disorganized and unstructured system. The church as an institution needs to organize itself to accomplish things in an orderly way, but it should focus more on people and relationships than on programs and hierarchies. The church has a head – Christ Jesus – at the top of the structure, and everything revolves around him. No gifted individual or charismatic person should claim the place of Christ. This is not to disregard the need for organized structure that enables a church to function. Without structures and forms the church community would be chaotic. The remedy is not to avoid structures but to ensure that the structures serve the purpose and the calling of the church. Julie Pomerleau writes this regarding a balanced approach:

> Maintaining a balance between the structure and community of the Church is important. The two must be 'organically united,' not seen as separate or opposing conceptions. The unique Church is at once heavenly and human, law and love, institution and fellowship, substantially divine but incorporated in humanity.[12]

This tension has to exist continually in the structure of the church. The structure should also focus on promoting Christ, connecting believers in discipleship and targeting the transformation of the wider community.

We should not underestimate the role of structures, despite their abuse in many institutions. If properly used, structures benefit the church immensely. The younger generation in many contemporary churches globally is not in favor of structures and existing establishments. The complaint is that structure puts people in boxes of leaders and followers, clergy and laity, and so on. But structure can be designed to facilitate fellowship and edification of believers and mission to the world in words and in deeds.

> If the church as a community of disciples is to be faithful to the gift of revelation and its historical expression, the church must attend to and nurture the creative interplay between charism and institution. Since both aspects of the social dimension function sacramentally as potentially revelatory of God's presence, they must be properly understood and fostered as an indispensable dimension of the messianic people of God.[13]

Mallon points out that the church's faithfulness to the Word of God can creatively structure itself and balance institution and charismatic leadership. The current inclination of the emerging apostolic churches in Africa and globally is to be flexible – the structure is decided by the charismatic leader. These churches are shaped after the founder and die with the leader. Gifted leaders are important for churches, but to depend on a single individual is not a healthy leadership style. Discipleship-focused structure equips and prepares members to serve not only the church but also the wider community.

In practice, the discipleship structure has to begin with the smallest unit of the society – the family. Individual believers have to be connected with their immediate families. If one does not have close family members it is good to connect the individual with other Christian families. Couples should see

---

12. Pomerleau, "Yves Congar's Ecclesiology," 17.
13. Mallon, *Traditioning Disciples*, 216.

each other as disciplers who are yoked together to grow and serve God as a family. If families fail to practice discipleship in their homes with their close relatives it would be difficult to take discipleship to the next level. Pastors and full-time ministers should make sure that every believer is connected to some kind of family relationship. Without discipleship in place in the basic family unit, all other levels will be on shaky ground. A convert must be evaluated not only on his or her performance on Sunday, but also on how they practically live out their faith in their respective families. The point of evaluation must be the degree of transformation – parents to godly parents, and spouses to godly spouses.

The second level for discipleship structure is a small group that meets in the neighborhood with fellow believers. Believers should demonstrate a strong presence in their neighborhood as they care for one another and their neighbors. A small group can serve as a support group as well as an accountability group. Personal struggles and challenges can be discussed openly as the believers grow together. These groups should organize themselves in discipleship groups in order to reach out to the neighborhood. It should not be an exclusive group where only believers enjoy their protected fellowship; it should be open to the community so that there are opportunities for others to hear the gospel.

The third level of discipleship structure is similar to the small group, but this is more for professionals at their work place. Whether one works with believers or non-believers it is important to have a group meeting with fellow workers as they unite to impact their workplace for Christ. For students, school fellowships help to mentor and disciple one another, and for professionals, workplace Bible study groups have the same function.

Fourth, ministry group fellowships in the local church can also be a good discipleship opportunity. People who are involved in the same ministry department, such as deacons, prayer leaders, elders, and choir groups, can shape their meetings to disciple each other. Ministry groups, rather than just focusing on the programs and activities, should also plan to grow together as they minister and disciple one another.

Finally, the local church level is where believers should gather to celebrate and fellowship as a culmination of all the discipleship structures. The spiritual growth takes place mainly in small groups but the larger group at the local church level is for public celebration. At the congregational level it is difficult to do much personal mentoring because of the larger group size. The sad fact is that many church members meet on Sunday morning but are not committed to any other small group structures.

When gatherings of God's people are structured as described above, the role of leadership is to facilitate and follow up with the group leaders. A leader has to be a disciple maker before he or she is an administrator or manager of a church. The leaders organize God's people according to their gifts so that they can function appropriately in the body of Christ. Every believer is part of the body of Christ and has a gift to contribute. Unfortunately, we see in the contemporary church that there are players and spectators, but everyone can be a player in the kingdom of God. Today in contexts like Africa many "faith preachers" and so-called gifted healers are treated as celebrities – as uniquely anointed agents of God with bodyguards and luxury cars. Lack of biblical discipleship structure has led the church of Christ to give in to all kinds of false teachings and practices.

Church Culture of Discipleship

Discipleship is a lifetime calling of the church. As individuals or groups of believers our calling is to follow Christ before anything else. For a church to exhibit a disciple-making culture it has to be in the DNA of the church tradition. It has to be more than a program or a practice of the church. A discipleship culture goes with the church's eternal calling. The question then is: How can we traditionalize discipleship and make it part of the culture of the church? It does not just happen; it takes the whole congregation to work together in developing a culture of discipleship. There is no "one size fits all" in developing the culture of discipleship, but I would like to mention the key players in the process.

Believers tend to complain about the culture or adopt it without discernment. Others blame the culture for all the spiritual struggles of the church. Many believers not only give up on the secular culture but also give up on the church tradition. There are many believers who prefer to stay at home and watch Christian television programs where they can passively attend the shows. They give up on the complicated structure and biased treatment of the members by the pastors or leaders of the church. Still others run from church to church searching for a perfect community without problems, only to be disappointed after a short while. Believers are to be convinced that they are called not just to complain about the church culture but to change it. Culture can be changed or recreated because it is dynamic not static. Andy Crouch rightly poses a question that the church should reflect on critically. He writes,

> I wonder what we Christians are known for in the world outside our churches. Are we known as critics, consumers, copiers, condemners of culture? I'm afraid so. Why aren't we known as cultivators – people who tend and nourish what is best in human culture, who do the hard and painstaking work to preserve the best of what people before us have done? Why aren't we known as creators – people who dare to think and do something that has never been thought or done before, something that makes the world more welcoming and thrilling and beautiful?[14]

Crouch draws his principle from the book of Genesis: humanity is created to care for creation and create new things. Similarly, Christians can cultivate the already existing positive cultural elements and create new ones based on the values of Scripture. Believers should intentionally aim to set the stage to create new culture that exhibits justice and peace in the community. This would not be introducing a culture from a different planet; it is introducing the kingdom of God in the day-to-day lives of people. For such a noble task of creating a discipleship culture, two main issues are crucial, namely, the process and the agents of culture creation.

First, the socialization of a believer is a key process in culture formation. Discipleship is a communal task. Establishing a community that embraces, informs and forms disciples is the primary step. Community formation is a contextual issue and it has to be done in a culturally relevant way. According to Boojamra, "socialization is a pattern of integrating new members as well as nurturing old members."[15] Integrating a believer into the body of Christ is the most important task in the beginning of the discipleship journey. This process continues as long as the church exists here on earth and continues to preach the gospel. In this process, a new convert begins to test and experience the new life in Christ. Boojamra strongly emphasizes the need for socialization to build a strong community. He writes, "People, both children and adults, become Christian not by learning about Christianity but by being integrated into an existing church through experiencing the rites and symbols of the community."[16] As noted above, individual lives are influenced more through

---

14. Crouch, "Creating Culture," 176.
15. Boojamra, "Socialization," 222.
16. Ibid., 220.

socialization than through formal instruction. This is not to play down the role of education in discipleship, rather to emphasize the reality of human experience, which involves the whole person, not just an intellect. In the contemporary context, proper socialization is not only a great need in the global church but also an urgent issue. One of the prominent leaders of the church in Nigeria describes the urgency when he writes, "If there is any time we need a culturally relevant discipling model such as Christian socialization, it is now. And it is now or never as we do not know when our Lord will return."[17] If the church fails to integrate new members into its community through discipleship it spreads negative experience that affects the witness of the church.

The socialization process has to reflect the culture and its training methodology. Some of the cultural methods of socialization and incorporation can be adapted to the Christian integration of new converts. The appropriate biblical ways of integrating believers into the body of Christ protect the church from unwanted fragmentation. Attempting to retain denominational distinctiveness undermines the kingdom concept and propagates interdenominational conflicts. Believers must be integrated into the local body of believers without neglecting the universal nature of the church.

According to Motty, Christian socialization should be critically contextualized, not copied from the secular culture. Christian socialization must be Bible-based, theocentric, Christ-focused, and relevant, with flexible and open-ended dialogue. Communities of discipleship have to be designed intentionally to focus on God and what Christ has done to bring people to fellowship. From the day a person first comes to church, he or she must be taught about the eternal calling of the church as a community. The foundation of the relationship has to be Christ and him alone. Relationships based on ethnic and racial similarities can negatively affect the unity of the church. The way the church is planted and organized has a lot to do with its continued operation and future direction.

According to Boojamra the socialization of new converts takes place in different stages, namely, externalization, objectification and internalization. At the externalization stage a convert feels like an outsider or stranger. The individual thinks and acts as a newcomer and observer. He or she is ready to copy what others are saying and doing. The community needs to be sensitive to people who are at this stage. At the objectification stage individuals begin to

---

17. Motty, *Indigenous Christian*, 201.

rationalize their actions. As they participate in rituals and services they begin to capture the basic concepts of the faith. At the final stage of internalization the converts begin to understand more deeply and become involved in what they have believed. For the process to be effective and productive, the church has to facilitate every stage of the socialization process and equip believers to negotiate it. When the process takes place in a natural and smooth way, the convert can easily integrate with the community – otherwise backsliding takes place.

Second, leaders are the main agents of culture creation in the Christian community. Leaders are responsible to set the standards and leave the legacy for the generation coming after them. The vision they set, the values they display, and the strategy they use in their leadership, all help to create a culture. Leaders should clearly understand the purpose of the church and communicate it clearly to the followers. Christian Breuninger writes,

> Founding leaders, like church planters, form culture. Pastors of newly developing churches embed culture. Pastors of mature churches maintain, reform, or bust culture. In all cases, the development of culture is a leadership dynamic that is done either intentionally or unintentionally.[18]

The challenge of this culture-making is that once the church has embraced the culture it is difficult to change. Many churches split over traditions and establishment. If the culture is a discipleship culture, where leaders and members are committed to make disciples, then except for adjusting to the contemporary culture there is no need to change. That is why the Bible calls for mature people to be leaders – because they set the culture of the church. Mature leaders not only create culture but also challenge and critique cultures. In many churches today leaders are not focused on creating discipleship culture but instead are distracted by many other administrative issues. Greg Ogden notes that "pastors are busy with caregiving duties instead of investing in leadership development, [they are] discipling individuals to maturity, . . . managing a ministry culture where people are ministering to one another or visiting parishioners in the work place."[19] Leaders are assigned to create a system and culture where the members connect with one another to take care of each other. Otherwise the routine would narrow the vision for their

---

18. Breuninger, "Creating a Culture," 15.

19. Ogden, *Transforming Discipleship*, 42.

leadership. Where there are no disciples, there are no ministers to care for the members and the leaders are obliged to carry the burden alone.

However, leadership without mature believers in the congregation cannot build a discipleship culture. Mature members who are disciples and are ready to make disciples are important in the culture-making business. Although new converts get religious instruction from church pastors and leaders, the actual living and modeling is done in a small group where people get closer to one another. Mature members in the congregation can help new members to be integrated into the discipleship system and create an ongoing culture. Before the new members meet the pastor, they meet the existing members in their vicinity. Before they hear the leaders, the converts listen to the closer members in the neighborhood. If the message they are hearing is contradictory, it retards the growth of the converts. This shows how the church needs to equip the entire membership towards making discipleship a culture, because every member is needed in this process.

Churches need leaders who can influence the world for Christ by modeling life in the market place. One of the weaknesses of the contemporary church is that the leaders equip their members to function well in the church context yet do not prepare them well to demonstrate their faith to the world beyond the church compound. In a discipleship culture believers are prepared to influence both the internal and external community. Otherwise, our efforts in evangelism are in vain. "Evangelism is incomplete if it rushes from "soul" to "soul" unconcerned whether the new convert grows, matures, and reproduces. It is not enough to have churches filled with people who are ready for heaven but not for earth."[20] The gospel brings transformation that is inside and outside, that is personal and communal. Sometimes, because of the lack of discipleship, the process of transformation is aborted, and stillborn believers fail to function properly in their specific contexts. Edgemon adds,

> Biblical discipleship does not lead one to withdraw from the world and view the study of discipleship as an end within itself. We are not to be introverted monks, disassociated from the ongoing program of an aggressive evangelistic ministry, but rather we are to be involved in the hurt, aches, loneliness, pain, and disillusionment of a world for whom Jesus died.[21]

---

20. Edgemon, "Evangelism," 544.
21. Ibid., 545.

Our presence in the world is both physical and spiritual. After we preach the gospel, we should demonstrate its power in the community. The church must present an alternative culture that refutes the fallen culture of humanity. The church is a new community with a new kingdom culture of discipleship at its core.

To establish a discipleship culture in the church requires a multidirectional approach. Education is at the center and the structure organizes the process in which discipleship becomes a culture of the church as it edifies its members and witnesses to the world.

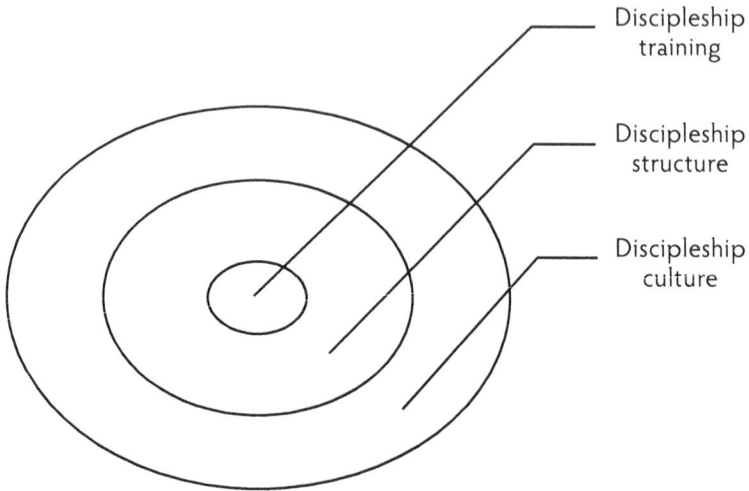

Figure 4. Multidirectional Approach to Discipleship

As illustrated above, at the core of the discipleship process is biblical teaching and the training of believers. Addressing the minds of believers to the transforming Word of God is foundational. The teaching has to be supported by the structures of the church. Leaders must prioritize discipleship as the primary calling of the church and as the duty to which they are assigned. Christ is at the center, and following him must be the focus of the church. This process has to be established as an essential aspect of the church's culture and tradition that continues from generation to generation. The church should approach discipleship from many angles to address the contemporary crisis that the churches are facing. Discipleship must become the foundation for any ministry of the church, whether it is among believers or non-believers. It is in and through a dedicated and committed approach to discipleship that the global church can bring genuine revival.

7

Discipleship, Mission and the Future of the Church

Without discipleship, the church will not accomplish its mission, and it will have no future. The truth of Christianity can only be transmitted by a proclamation that is accompanied by a strong demonstration. Discipleship is the future for the survival of Christianity. The early church survived because of its strong discipleship program and the current global church will survive the challenge of the secular culture through strong strategic discipleship. Church growth without discipleship should concern us because it would be like a house built on the sand without a foundation. Whether it is in the declining Western church or the striving non-Western church, discipleship is the way to go to impact the world with the gospel. Galgalo doubts the future of Christianity in Africa if the church fails to disciple its members. He writes,

> As history has proved twice over already, but more so going by plenty of signs already at hand, it is likely that the present day vibrant Christianity may have seen its better days and it could be only a matter of time before it goes the way of the African Christianity of the earlier phases. The fact of its shaky foundation is not in doubt.[1]

Galgalo predicts that the vibrant and growing church in Africa will not only stop growing but it will die if there is no discipleship. Discipleship is not a matter of choice, it is a matter of necessity.

The global church of Christ should work together closely to establish a culture of discipleship in every context. Denominations, parachurch organizations and mission institutions should cooperate towards this one

---

1. Galgalo, *African Christianity*, 12.

goal which will define the future of the global church of Christ. Training institutions, theological seminaries and church education programs must all gear up towards producing faithful disciples to influence the corrupted world. Leaders should not be satisfied with the present number of converts but should work hard to organize every believer into a system where they can each be disciples. The dwindling of its members is an obvious sign of a dying church, but the lack of discipleship is a more subtle mark. The solution Jesus proposed is making disciples. It worked for the early Christians and it is working today and it will work for the future. As Collinson writes,

> Discipling has the authority of Jesus as being the model to be used for taking his message to the world. It is not optional. It is mandatory. As a model of teaching its value cannot be estimated too highly. Its distinctive strength lies in the formation of discipling communities of faith wherever the gospel is spread.[2]

The hope of Christianity is not in its politically motivated adherents or wealthy members who can influence the world through their resources; it is at the hands of ordinary believers who have made Christ their Lord and savior and are committed to its cause as disciples.

Today, Christian mission is facing extremely strong opponents such as secularism, violent Islamism and nominalism that all threaten to weaken the impact of Christianity. These are difficult days in which to do mission. Mission is increasingly losing its popularity and easily makes one politically incorrect. The times are getting more difficult as we approach the second coming of Christ. The future of mission is in the hands of disciples who are willing to take up their cross and follow Christ despite the circumstances. To prepare the church for the daunting task of mission in the future there is no way around other than making disciples of Christ everywhere.

Conclusion

Christianity today is facing challenges from both within and without. The churches that are growing have weak foundations because of the lack of discipleship. Many other churches are struggling to keep Christ, the head of the church, at the center. Christianity without discipleship, theology without life transformation, and a church without kingdom community are hurting

---

2. Collinson, *Making Disciples*, 176.

the mission of the church. The solution is a comprehensive and integrative approach in which the ministries of the church work in coordination with each other to strengthen the unity of the church and equip it for the mission given by God.

The primary task of the church that is commanded and modeled by Christ is to makes disciples – not just members, not even world-known scholars or celebrities. Disciples are people who follow Christ, obeying his words, and make others disciples of Christ. Discipleship is a journey that requires a strong foundation, adequate equipment to overcome the challenges, and a community that accompanies on the journey. Contextualization sets the stage in communicating the gospel, making clear the message that changes individual lives, and organizing the community in culturally appropriate structures with biblical foundations. All this brings transformation in the wider community as God is glorified and his kingdom extended. In Figure 5 below, the horizon gets bigger and bigger as believers continue to understand the message, live Christ-like lives individually, and serve as light and salt in the community.

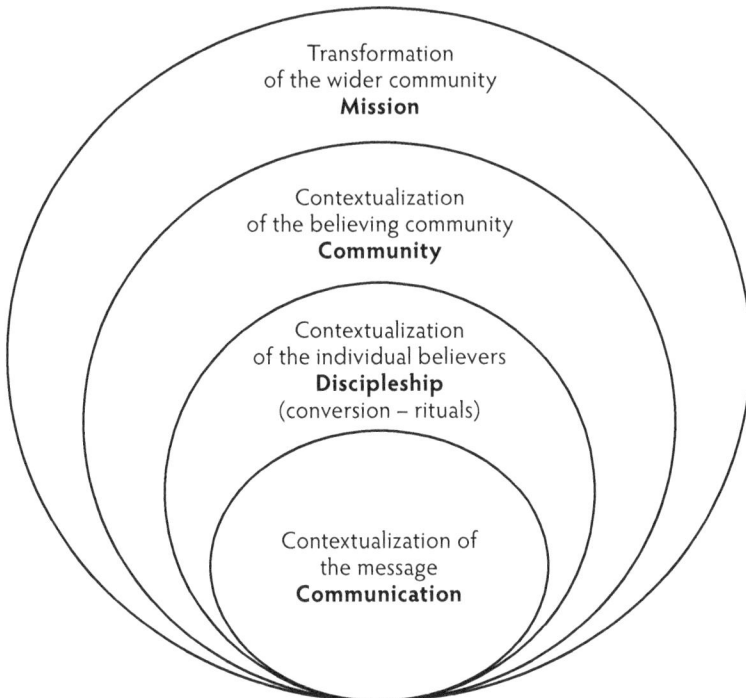

Figure 5. Transformative Contextualized Discipleship

The integrative approach assumes a continual dialogue between the community and its context, between the culture and the message of the gospel, and between the individual and the community. As the dialogue continues both the individual believer and the church community grow towards the likeness of Christ and bring a significant impact on the society. Therefore, contextualization should target discipleship and discipleship should focus on the mission of God.

References

Adams, Lane. *The Incredible Patience of God*. Maitland, FL: Xulon Press, 2013.

Aghiorgoussis, Maximos. "The Meaning of Christian Baptism for the Baptized and for the Church." *Greek Orthodox Theological Review* 55 (2010): 1–4.

Alston, Wallace M. *The Church of the Living God*. Louisville, KY: Westminster John Knox Press, 2002.

Anderson, Herbert. "How Rituals Heal." *Word and World* 30, no. 1 (2010).

Arias, Mortimer. "Church in the World." *Theology Today* 47, no. 4 (1991): 410–418.

Ashford, Bruce R. *Theology and Practice of Mission*. Nashville, TN: B&H Academic, 2011.

Bakke, Johnny. *Christian Ministry: Patterns & Functions within the Ethiopian Evangelical Church Mekane Yesus*. Atlantic Highlands, NJ: Humanities Press, 1987.

Balisky, Paul. *Wolaitta Evangelists*. Eugene, OR: Pickwick, 2009.

Barna, George. *Growing True Disciples: New Strategies for Producing Genuine Followers of Christ*. Colorado Springs, CO: Waterbrook Press, 2001.

Barrett, David. "Annual Statistical Table on Global Mission." *International Bulletin of Missionary Research* 18, no. 1 (1997): 25.

Bediako, Kwame. *Christianity in Africa: The Renewal of Non-Western Religion*. Edinburgh: University Press, 1995.

Bekele, Girma. *The In-Between People*. Eugene, OR: Pickwick Publications, 2011.

Belete, Getachew. *Elohe Ena Hale Luya*. Addis Ababa: The EKHC Literature Dep., 2000.

Bilezikian, Gilbert. *Community 101: Reclaiming the Local Church as Community of Oneness*. Grand Rapids, MI: Zondervan, 1997.

Bonhoeffer, Dietrich. *The Cost of Discipleship*. New York: MacMillan, 1959.

———. *Discipleship*. Minneapolis, MN: Fortress Press, 2001.

Boojamra, John L. "Socialization as a Historic Model for Christian Integration." *St. Vladimir's Theological Quarterly* 25, no. 4 (1981): 219–237.

Bosch, David. *Transforming Mission*. Maryknoll, NY: Orbis Books, 1991.

Breuninger, Christian B. "Creating a Culture of Mission in the Church." *The Covenant Quarterly* 56, no. 2 (1998).

Brook, Wes Howard, and Sharon H. Ringe. *The New Testament: Introducing the Way of Discipleship*. Maryknoll, NY: Orbis Books, 2002.

Buckser, Andrew, and Stephen D. Glazier. *The Anthropology of Religious Conversion*. New York: Rowman and Littlefield, 2003.

Burton, William L. "Baptism in the New Testament." *Bible Today* 53, no. 4 (2015): 223–266.

Chai, Teresa. "A Look at Contextualization: Historical Background, Definition, Function, Scope and Models." *Asian Journal of Pentecostal Studies* 18, no. 1 (2015): 3–19.

Chang, E., and J. R. Morgan, et al. "Paul G. Hiebert and Critical Contextualization." *Trinity Journal* 30, no. 2 (2009): 199–207.

Chidester, David. *Christianity: A Global History*. San Francisco, CA: Harper, 2000.

———. "The Challenge to Christian Ritual Studies." *Anglican Theological Review,* 2006.

Chitando, Ezra. *Inculturation and Postcolonial Discourse in African Theology*. Edited by Edward P. Antonio. New York: Peter Lang, 2006.

Collinson, Sylvia Wilkey. *Making Disciples: The Significance of Jesus' Educational Methods for Today's Church*. Carlisle: Paternoster Press, 2004.

Conn, Walter. *Christian Conversion: A Developmental Interpretation of Autonomy and Surrender*. New York: Paulist Press, 1986.

Cooke, Bernard, and Gary Macy. *Christian Symbol and Rituals: An Introduction*. Oxford: Oxford University Press, 2005.

Cope, Landa. "His Kingdom Come." In *His Kingdom Come: An Integrated Approach to Discipling the Nations and Fulfilling the Great Commission*, edited by Jim Stier and Richlyn Poor. Seattle, WA: YWAM Publishing, 2008.

———. *An Introduction to the Old Testament Template*. Seattle, WA: YWAM Publishing, 2011.

Cotterell, Peter F. *Born at Midnight*. Chicago, IL: Moody Press, 1973.

Courson, Jim. "Deepening the Bonds of Christian Community." *Missiology* 26, no. 3 (1998): 301–313.

Couturier, David B. *The Four Conversions: A Spirituality of Transformation*. South Bend, IN: Victoria Press, 2008.

Crouch, Andy. "Creating Culture." *Christianity Today* 52, no. 9 (2008): 24–29.

Deflem, Mathieu. "Ritual, Anti-Structure and Religion: A Discussion of Victor Turner's Processual Symbolic Analysis." *Journal for the Scientific Study of Religion* 30, no. 1 (1991): 1–25.

Degefa, Lemma. *ECFE Missions Research*. Addis Ababa: Rehoboth Printing, 2005.

De Ridder, Richard. *Discipling the Nations*. Grand Rapids, MI: Baker Books, 1975.

Dodson, Jonathan K. *Gospel Centered Discipleship*. Wheaton, IL: Crossway, 2012.

Driscoll, Mark. *Who Do You Think You Are?: Finding Your True Identity in Christ*. Nashville, TN: Thomas Nelson, 2013.

Driver, Tom F. *The Magic of Ritual*. San Francisco, CA: Harper, 1991.

Dueck, Irma F. "It's Only Water: The Ritual of Baptism and the Formation of Christian Identity." *Vision* 12, no. 2 (2011): 21–27.

Dunahoo, Charles H. *Making Kingdom Disciples: A New Framework*. Phillipsburg, NJ: P&R, 2005.

Edgemon, Roy T. "Evangelism and Discipleship." *Review and Expositor* 77, no. 4 (1980): 539–547.

Eide, Oyvind M. *Revolution and Religion in Ethiopia: The Growth and Persecution of the Mekane Yesus Church 1974–85*. Oxford: James Currey, 2000.

Eliade, Mircea. *Patterns of Comparative Religion*. New York: Sheed & Ward, 1958.

Eshete, Tibebe. *The Evangelical Movement in Ethiopia: Resistance and Resilience.* Waco, TX: Baylor University Press, 2009.

Etuk, Udo. "The Theology of Contextualization in Africa: A Cover for Traditional Cultural Revival." *Concordia Journal* 11, no. 6 (1985): 214–222.

Fargher, Brian L. *The Origin of the New Churches Movement in Southern Ethiopia, 1927–1944.* Leiden, NL: E. J. Brill, 1996.

Federal Democratic Republic of Ethiopia Population Census Commission 2008. Summary and Report of the 2007 Population and Housing Census Result. Printed by United Nation Population Fund (UNFPA). Addis Ababa.

Fernandez, Enrique. "Engaging Contextual Realities in Theological Education: Systems and Strategies." *ERT* 38, no. 14 (2014): 339–349.

Finn, Thomas M. "Ritual Process and the Survival of Early Christianity: A Study of the Apostolic Tradition of Hippolytus." *Journal of Ritual Studies* 3, no. 1 (1989): 69–89.

Foster, Paul. *Community, Law and Mission in Matthew's Gospel.* Tübingen, Germany: Mohr Siebeck, 2004.

Freeman, Dena. "Pentecostalism in a Rural Context: Dynamics of Religion and Development in Southwest Ethiopia." *PentcoStudies* 12, no. 2 (2013): 231–249.

Galgalo, Joseph. *African Christianity: The Stranger Within.* Limuru, Kenya: Zapf Chancery, 2012.

Garrison, Alton. *The 360 Disciples.* Springfield, MI: Gospel Publishing, 2004.

Gillespie, V. Bailey. *The Dynamics of Religious Conversion: Identity and Transformation.* Birmingham, AL: Religious Education Press, 1991.

———. *Religious Conversion and Personal Identity: How and Why People Change.* Birmingham, AL: Religious Education Press, 1979.

Gooren, Henri. *Religious Conversion and Disaffiliation: Tracing Patterns of Change in Faith Practices.* NY: Palgrave Macmillan, 2010.

Hartog, Paul. *The Contemporary Church and the Early Church: Case Studies in Resourcement.* Eugene, OR: Pickwick, 2010.

Hesselgrave, David J., and Edward Rommen. *Contextualization: Meanings, Methods, and Models.* Grand Rapids, MI: Baker Books, 1989.

Hiebert, Paul G. "Critical Contextualization." *Missiology: An International Review* 12, no. 3 (July 1984).

———. "Conversion in Cross-Cultural Perspective." In *Conversion: Doorway to Discipleship*, edited by H. J. Schmidt. Hillsboro, KS: Mennonite Brethren Publishing, 1980.

Hirsch, Alan, and Debra Hirsch. *Untamed: Reactivating a Missional Form of Discipleship.* Grand Rapids, MI: Baker Books, 2010.

Houston, James M. *The Disciples: Following the True Mentor.* Colorado Springs, CO: David Cook, 2007.

Hunter, George II. *The Celtic Way of Evangelism.* Nashville, TN: Abingdon, 2000.

Hussein, Jeylan W. "The Politics of Language, Power and Pedagogy in Ethiopia." *Australian Journal of Linguistics* 28, no. 1 (2008): 31–57.

Idleman, Kyle. *Not a Fan: What Does It Really Mean to Follow Jesus?* Grand Rapids, MI: Zondervan, 2011.

Ingleby, Jonathan. *Beyond Empire*. Milton Keynes, UK: Author House, 2010.

Jetter, Von Werner. *Symbol and Rituals*. Gottingen: Vanden Hoeck & Rupercht, 1986.

Kankanamalage, Indunil. "Conversion and Proselytism in the Light of 'Christian Witness in a Multi-Religious World.'" *International Review of Mission* 103, no. 1 (2014): 109–115.

Kapolyo, Joe. "Matthew." In *Africa Bible Commentary*, edited by Tokunboh Adeyemo, 1170. Nairobi, Kenya: World Alive, 2006.

Kasdorf, Hans. *Christian Conversion in Context*. Scottdale, PA: Herald Press, 1980.

Keener, Craig S. "Matthew's Missiology: Making Disciples of the Nations (Matt 28:19–20)." *Asian Journal of Pentecostal Studies* 12, no. 1 (2009): 3–20.

Keller, Timothy. *Center Church*. Grand Rapids, MI: Zondervan, 2012.

Kim, Dong Young. *Understanding Religious Conversion: The Case of Saint Augustine*. Eugene, OR: Pickwick, 2012.

Köstenberger, Andreas J. "Review of *The Discipleship Paradigm* by David R. Beck." *Journal of the Evangelical Theological Society* 42, no. 4 (1998): 749–751.

Kraft, Charles, ed. *Appropriate Christianity*. Pasadena, CA: William Carey, 2005.

Kwiyani, Harvey C. *Sent Forth: African Missionary Work in the West*. Maryknoll, NY: Orbis Books, 2014.

Launhardt, Johannes. *Evangelicals in Addis Ababa* (1919–1991). Münster: Lit Verlag, 2004.

Lawler, Michael G. "Christian Rituals: An Essay in Sacrament Symbolisms." *Horizons* 7, no. 1 (1980): 7–35.

Ligon, Bill, and Robert Paul Lamb. *Discipleship: The Jesus View*. Plainfield, NJ: Logos International, 1979.

Longo, Gregory, and Jungmeen Kim-Spoon. "What Drives Apostates and Converts." *Psychology of Religion* 6, no. 4 (2014): 284–291.

Lukken, Gerard. *Rituals in Abundance: Critical Reflections on the Place, Form and Identity of Christian Rituals in Our Culture*. Dudley, MA: Peters, 2005.

Mallon, Colleen Mary. *Traditioning Disciples: The Contribution of Cultural Anthropology to Ecclesial Identity*. Eugene, OR: Pickwick, 2010.

Malony, Newton H., and Samuel Southard, eds. *Handbook of Religious Conversion*. Birmingham, AL: Religious Education Press, 1992.

Mamo, Ermias. "Knowing God in Ritual Context in Special Reference to the Hamar People of Southern Ethiopia." Doctor of Philosophy Dissertation, Fuller Theological Seminary School of Intercultural Studies, 2008.

McCallum, Dennis, and Jessica Lowery. *Organic Discipleship: Mentoring Others into Spiritual Maturity and Leadership*. Houston, TX: Touch Publications, 2006.

McDonagh, Enda. *Church and Politics: From Theology to a Case History of Zimbabwe.* Notre Dame, IN: University of Notre Dame Press, 1980.

McDonough, Tim. "Initiation, Not Indoctrination: Confronting the Grotesque in Cultural Education." *Educational Philosophy and Theory* 43, no. 7 (2011).

Meeks, Wayne A. *The First Urban Christians: The Social World of the Apostle Paul.* New Haven, CT: Yale University Press, 1983.

Mengiste Ab, "The Church in Ethiopia Is in Danger!" *Mathetes.* Addis Ababa, Ethiopia, 2013.

Michael, Matthew. "African Theology and the Paradox of Missions: Three Intellectual Responses to the Modern Mission Crisis of the African Church." *Transformation* 31, no. 2 (2014): 79–98.

Miller, Randolph C. "Religious Education IX Yale University." ATLA series, 1968.

Moreau, Scott. "Contextualization That Is Comprehensive." *Missiology* 34, no. 3 (2006): 325–335.

———. *Contextualization in World Missions: Mapping and Assessing Evangelical Models.* Grand Rapids, MI: Kregel Academic, 2012.

Motty, Bauta D. *Indigenous Christian Disciple-Making.* Jos, Plateau State: ECWA Publications, 2013.

Muriti, Susan. "Contextual Theological Education in Africa as a Model for missional Formation." *The Asbury Journal* 69, no. 2 (2014).

Murphy-O'Connor, Jerome. *Becoming Human Together: The Pastoral Anthropology of St. Paul.* Atlanta, GA: Society of Biblical Literature, 2009.

Obijole, Olubayo. "The Church and the Gospel Message in the African Cultural Context." *Ogbomoso Journal of Theology* 17, no. 1 (2012): 105.

Ogden, Greg. *Transforming Discipleship: Making Disciples a Few at a Time.* Downers Grove, IL: InterVarsity Press, 2003.

Onwubiko, Oliver Alozie. *The Church in Mission in the Light of Ecclesia in Africa.* Nairobi, Kenya: Paulines Publication, 2001.

Ortiz, Juan Carlos. *Disciple.* Carol Stream, IL: Creation House, 1975.

Paloutzian, Raymond, James Richardson, and Lewis Rambo et al. "Religious Conversion and Personality Change." *Journal of Personality* 67, no. 6 (1999): 1047–1079.

Park, Timothy K., and Steve K. Eom, eds. *Discipleship in the 21st Century Mission.* Kyonggi, Korea: East-West Centre for Mission Research & Development, 2011.

Pomerleau, Julie M. "Yves Congar's Ecclesiology and the Role of the Church in the World." *Journal of Theta Alpha Kappa* 38, no. 2 (2014): 13–35.

Rambo, Lewis R. *Understanding Religious Conversion.* New Haven, CT: Yale University Press, 1993.

Rench, Craig Wesley. *The Master's Plan: A Strategy for Making Disciples.* Kansas City, MO: Beacon Hill Press, 2011.

Rooms, Nigel. "Theological Education in a New Missional Era." *Dialog: A Journal of Theology* 53, no. 4 (December 2014): 336–344.

Samra, James G. "A Biblical View of Discipleship." *Bibliotheca Sacra* 160 (2003): 219–234.

Sanchez, Daniel R. "Theological and Practical Lessons to Be Learned from the Small Church." *Review and Expositor* 93 (1996): 357–367.

Schmidt, Henry J., ed. *Conversion: Doorway to Discipleship.* Hillsboro, KS: Mennonite Brethren Publishing, 1980.

Segal, Robert A. "Victor Turner's Theory of Ritual." *Zygon* 18, no. 3 (1983): 327–335.

Sharkey, Heather J. *Cultural Conversions: Unexpected Consequences of Christian Missionary Encounters in the Middle East, Africa, and South Asia.* Syracuse, NY: Syracuse University Press, 2013.

Shaw, Daniel R. "Beyond Contextualization: Toward a Twenty-First Century Model for Enabling Mission." *International Bulletin of Missionary Research* 34, no. 4 (2010): 208–215.

Shirley, Chris. "It Takes a Church to Make a Disciple." *Southwestern Journal of Theology* 50, no. 2 (2008): 207–223.

Smith, Gordon T. *Beginning Well: Christian Conversion & Authentic Transformation.* Downers Grove, IL: InterVarsity Press, 2001.

Smith, Justin. "Missional Communities and Community Foundation." *Missio Apolostica,* 2013.

Snyder, Howard A. *The Community of the King.* Downers Grove, IL: InterVarsity, 1977.

Song, Minho. "Contextualization and Discipleship: Closing the Gap between Theory and Practice." *Evangelical Review of Theology* 30, no. 3 (2006): 249–263.

Spindler, Marc R. "Conversion Revisited: Present Understanding of a Classic Missionary Motive." *Missiology: An International Review* 25, no. 3 (1997): 293–295.

Stier, Jim, and Richlyn Poor, eds. *His Kingdom Come: An Integrated Approach to Discipling the Nations and Fulfilling the Great Commission.* Seattle, WA: YWAM Publishing, 2008.

Sunquist, Scott. *The Unexpected Christian Century: The Reversal and Transformation of Global Christianity, 1900–2000.* Grand Rapids, MI: Baker Academic, 2015.

Swanson, Allen J. "Decision or Disciples?" *Missiology: An International Review* 17, no. 1 (Jan 1989).

———. *Mending the Nets.* Pasadena, CA: William Carey, 1986.

Tolo, Arne. *Sidama and Ethiopian: The Emergence of the Mekane Yesus Church in Sidama.* Uppsala: Uppsala University Press, 1998.

Turner, Victor W. *The Ritual Process: Structure and Anti-structure.* Chicago, IL: Aldine Publishing, 1969.

Urga, et al. "Ethiopian and the Mission of God." Unpublished manuscript, 2015.

Van Gennep, Arnold. *The Rites of Passage.* Chicago, IL: University of Chicago Press, 1975.

Wahl, W. P. "Towards Relevant Theological Education in Africa." *Actea Theologica* 33, no. 1 (2013): 266–293.

Walls, Andrew F. "The Significance of Global Christianity for Theological Education and Scholarship." *Ogbomoso Journal of Theology* 15, no. 1 (2010): 1–10.

Wells, David F. *Turning to God: Biblical Conversion in the Modern World*. Grand Rapids, MI: Baker Books, 1989.

West, Richard, and Dan Noel. "Situational Discipleship: The Fivefold Ministry Roles of Ephesians 4:11 and Their Relationship to the Situational Leadership Model." *Culture and Religion Review Journal* 3 (2013): 124–144.

Wilder, Terry L. "A Biblical Theology of Missions and Contextualization." *Southwestern Journal of Theology* 55, no. 1 (2012): 3–17.

Wilkins, Michael J. *Discipleship in the Ancient World and Matthew's Gospel*. Grand Rapids, MI: Baker Books, 1995.

Wright, Christopher J. H. *The Mission of God*. Downers Grove, IL: InterVarsity, 2006.

Zahniser, A. H. Mathias. *Symbol and Ceremony*. Pasadena, CA: MARC, 1997.

———. "Ritual Process and Christian Discipling: Contextualizing a Buddhist Rite of Passage." *Missiology: An International Review* 19, no. 1 (1991): 3–19.

Lightning Source UK Ltd.
Milton Keynes UK
UKHW020658281021
392934UK00007B/88

9 781783 683659